INDOOR GRILL COOKBOOK FOR BEGINNERS

101 Indoor Grill and Air Fryer Recipes, The Ultimate Starter Guide!

INTRODUCTION

While some things are too good to be true, believe me when I say you can enjoy the taste of summer BBQs year-round with the Indoor Grill! Bring the outside flavors of classic char-grilled days spent by the pool into the comfort and convenience of your own kitchen. The Indoor Grill gives you those characteristic grill marks that just have a way of making food taste better.

If indoor grilling wasn't enough, you've also just added an air fryer into your life! Air frying is all the rage and for good reason. If you ever thought that fried and healthy were descriptors that could not possibly exist within the same sentence, air frying is about to blow your mind. Air fryers allow you to crisp up your favorite foods with just a tiny bit of oil allowing you to prepare perfectly spiced fried potatoes or the satisfying crunch of thick onion rings, with 75% less guilt.

The time spent preparing a solid meal for yourself or an entire family is often a chore from both the physical effort exerted and the need to plan ahead and properly thaw frozen ingredients as needed. And there is no horror greater than sitting in evening traffic on your way home with the realization that you forgot to take the chicken out of the freezer before you left for work. This grill removes that negativity you just don't need in your life by taking your frozen foods, be it vegetables or meat, and transforming them into a perfectly cooked meal in no time.

Not to mention, you never have to brave the freezing cold or the dreadful heat just to enjoy a good meal. Everything can be prepared from the convenience of your kitchen and clean-up is a breeze. This virtually smokeless option is sure to please roommates, landlords, and anyone who is lucky enough to be eating at home that night!

From warm and hearty breakfasts and late-night indulgences, to juicy, tender steaks and a melty pie for pizza night, we've got you covered so you can start enjoying the newest addition to your kitchen in no time!

BOOKS ON DECK

CONTENTS

Breakfast

Chicken

Beef

Pork, Lamb & Veal

Fish & Seafood

Burgers & Sausages

Pizza

Vegetables & Sides

Appetizers & Snacks

Desserts

Bacon

Breakfast

Whether it's the weekend or a bright and early weekday morning, nothing quite starts the day like a complete breakfast. With your new Indoor Grill making time for that morning meal is no longer a luxury reserved for those with an abundance of time in the morning! Let's eat some breakfast!

1. Grilled Cheese & Avocado Sandwich

Level: Simple/Beginner | Function: Grill | Prep: 10 mins | Preheat: 8 mins |
Cook: 4 mins | Makes: 2 – 4

INGREDIENTS:

2 tbsp high smoke point oil

4 slices whole-grain bread

4 slices Gruyere cheese

½ ripe avocado, peeled and cut into strips

¼ cup grated Swiss cheese and sliced

DIRECTIONS:

1. Insert the grill grate into the Indoor Grill and close the lid. Select Grill, set the temperature to Max, and the time to 4 minutes. Press Start/Stop to initiate preheating.

2. Brush the oil on one side of each bread side. Place the two bread slices on a flat plate (with oiled sides down) and lay 2 slices of Gruyere cheese on each. Divide the avocado strips on top, sprinkle the Swiss cheese on the avocado, and cover with the other 2 bread slices with oiled sides up.

3. Once the Indoor Grill has preheated, carefully place the sandwiches on the grate, close the lid, and cook until the timer is up.

4. When ready, transfer the sandwiches to a chopping board, diagonally slice in halves, and enjoy!

☆☆☆☆☆
Rating

Notes:

----

2. Foil Grilled Potatoes with Bacon and Cheese

Level: Simple/Beginner | Function: Grill | Prep: 10 mins | Preheat: 8 mins |
Cook: 25 mins | Makes: 2 – 4

INGREDIENTS:

1 lb Russet potatoes, cleaned and cut into 1-inch pieces

1 ½ tbsp ranch seasoning mix (powder)

4 tbsp melted salted butter

1 tbsp high smoke point oil

1 cup grated Monterey Jack cheese

6 bacon slices, cooked and crumbled (see recipe 101)

Sour cream for topping

2 tbsp chopped fresh scallions for garnishing

DIRECTIONS:

1. Insert the grill grate into the Indoor Grill and close the lid. Select Grill, set the temperature to Max, and the time to 25 minutes. Press Start/Stop to initiate preheating.

2. In a large bowl, mix the potatoes, ranch seasoning, butter, and oil until the potatoes are well-coated with the seasoning.

3. Cut out 2 large rectangles out of heavy-duty foil and lay both on a flat surface. Divide the potatoes onto the foil and fold the sides of the foil over the potatoes, but do not squeeze to seal.

4. Once the Indoor Grill has preheated, open the lid and place the foil packets on top. Close the lid and grill for 15 minutes. Open the lid, open the foil using tongs or utensils (it will be hot!) and check the potatoes for doneness (should be fork tender) ; cook further for 5 minutes if necessary.

5. When the potatoes are done, use tongs or utensils to open the packets and scatter the cheese and bacon on top. Cover the foil over the topping but don't seal the packets. Close the lid and cook further for 3 to 5 minutes or until the cheese melts.

6. Transfer the packets onto serving plates, open widely, and top with the sour cream and chives.

7. Serve warm.

☆☆☆☆☆
Rating

Notes:

----

3. Cinnamon Toast Sticks with Berries and Whipped Cream

Level: Simple/Beginner | Function: Air Crisp | Prep: 10 mins | Preheat: 3 mins |
Cook: 10 mins | Makes: 4

INGREDIENTS:

2 large eggs

1 tbsp melted butter

1/3 cup full-fat milk

1 tsp vanilla extract

2 tsp confectioner's sugar

2 tbsp fresh orange zest

8 slices day-old bread, cut into thirds

Sugar mix topping:

½ cup brown sugar

¼ tsp nutmeg powder

1 tsp cinnamon powder

Other toppings:

Maple syrup

Whipped cream

1 to 1 ½ cups fresh raspberries (or sliced strawberries) and blueberries

DIRECTIONS:

1. Crack the eggs into a medium bowl and whisk with the butter, milk, vanilla, confectioner's sugar, and orange zest.

2. Dip in the bread strips and turn once or twice to coat thoroughly in the egg mixture. Allow sitting for 3 minutes while you preheat the Indoor Grill.

3. Insert the crisper basket into the Indoor Grill and close the lid. Select Air Crisp, set the temperature to 375°F, the timer to 10 minutes, and press Start/Stop to initiate preheating.

4. Meanwhile, in a small bowl, mix the brown sugar, nutmeg powder, and cinnamon powder. Transfer the bread from the egg mix onto a wide plate (while dripping off as much egg mix as possible) and sprinkle the sugar mix on both sides of the bread.

5. When the Indoor Grill is preheated, arrange the bread in the crisper basket. Close the lid and cook for 10 minutes while shaking the basket after 5 minutes.

6. When the cooking time is done, check the toast sticks for doneness;, cook further for 2 minutes if needed.

7. Once ready, transfer to 4 serving plates and generously swirl maple syrup on top. Press on some whipped cream and scatter the berries on top.

8. Serve immediately.

☆☆☆☆☆
Rating

Notes:

----

4. Mushroom and Spinach Egg Muffins

Level: Simple/Beginner | Function: Bake | Prep: 10 mins | Preheat: 3 mins |
Cook: 15 mins | Makes: 4

ACCESSORIES:

8 silicone muffin cups

INGREDIENTS:

½ cup cremini mushrooms, finely chopped

½ cup minced mixed bell peppers

2 garlic cloves, minced

1 small yellow onion, minced

1 small tomato, finely chopped

2 tbsp chopped fresh scallions

1 cup fresh baby spinach, chopped

4 whole eggs

4 egg whites

Sea salt and black pepper to taste

½ cup grated cheddar cheese

DIRECTIONS:

1. Insert the cooking pot into the Indoor Grill and close the lid. Select Bake, set the temperature to 300°F, the time to 15 minutes, and press Start/Stop to initiate preheating.

2. In a medium bowl, mix the mushrooms, bell peppers, garlic, onion, tomato, and scallions. Evenly divide the mixture into the muffin cups and top with the spinach.

3. Crack the eggs into the bowl and whisk with the egg whites, salt, and black pepper. Evenly pour the mixture into the muffin cups and sprinkle the cheddar cheese on top.

4. When the Indoor Grill is preheated, open the lid and carefully arrange the muffin cups in the cooking pot. Close the lid and cook for 15 minutes.

5. When ready, open the lid, insert a toothpick into a muffin to check for doneness, if not done, cook further for 2 minutes.

6. Transfer the muffin cups to a flat surface and serve after they cool.

☆☆☆☆☆
Rating

Notes:

----

5. Sundried Tomato and Bacon Frittata

Level: Simple/Beginner | Function: Bake | Prep: 10 mins | Preheat: 3 mins |
Cook: 20 mins | Makes: 4 – 6

INGREDIENTS:

8 large eggs

¼ tsp garlic powder

½ tsp onion powder

¼ cup half and half

Sea salt and black pepper to taste

10 bacon slices, cooked and crumbled

1 cup sundried tomatoes, chopped

1 (7 oz) can sliced mushrooms, drained

1 tbsp high smoke point oil

2/3 cup grated Gruyere cheese

1 tbsp chopped fresh chives for garnish

DIRECTIONS:

1. Insert the cooking pot into the Indoor Grill and close the lid. Select Bake, set the temperature to 325°F, the time to 20 minutes, and press Start/Stop to initiate preheating.

2. Crack the eggs into a medium bowl and whisk with the garlic powder, onion powder, half and half, salt, and black pepper. Mix in the bacon, tomatoes, and mushrooms until evenly distributed.

3. When the Indoor Grill is preheated, open the lid, brush or spray the pot with the oil, pour the mixture into the cooking pot, and sprinkle the cheese on top. Close the lid and cook for 15 minutes.

4. After 15 minutes, open the lid, insert a toothpick into the frittata to check for doneness, cook further for 5 minutes if needed.

5. With oven mitts, open the lid and remove the cooking pot. Allow the frittata cool for 2 minutes and run a spatula around the edges of the frittata to release from the pot. Carefully, slide the frittata onto a wide plate and garnish with the chives.

6. Slice the food and serve warm.

☆☆☆☆☆
Rating

Notes:

_____

_____

_____

_____

_____

6. Rosemary Potatoes and Sausage Breakfast Hash

Level: Simple/Beginner | Function: Grill | Prep: 15 mins | Preheat: 8 mins | Cook: 27 mins | Makes: 4

INGREDIENTS:

4 Russet potatoes, cleaned, peeled and sliced into 1-inch rounds

1 large green bell pepper, deseeded and cut into quarters

1 large red bell pepper, deseeded and cut into quarters

½ tsp onion powder

½ tsp garlic powder

1 tsp dried rosemary

1 tsp paprika

12 sausage links

Salt and black pepper to taste

1 tbsp chopped fresh parsley

DIRECTIONS:

1. Insert the grill grate into the Indoor Grill and close the lid. Select Grill, set the temperature to Max, and the time to 15 minutes. Press Start/Stop to initiate preheating.

2. In a medium bowl, toss the potatoes and bell peppers with the onion powder, garlic powder, rosemary, and paprika.

3. When the Indoor Grill has preheated, open the lid and arrange the potatoes and bell peppers on the grill grate. Close the lid and cook for 15 minutes, flipping is not necessary.

4. Once ready, transfer to a plate or bowl and set aside.

5. Reduce the Indoor Grill's temperature to Low, set the time to 12 minutes, and arrange the sausages on top. Close the lid and cook for 12 minutes. No need to flip.

6. Remove and chop up the sausages then combine with the potatoes and bell peppers in a medium bowl. Season with a little salt, black pepper, and toss well.

7. Dish the food onto 4 serving plates, garnish with the parsley, and serve immediately.

☆☆☆☆☆
Rating

Notes:

----

7. Cornbread with Butter and Syrup

Level: Simple/Beginner | Function: Bake | Prep: 7 mins | Preheat: 3 mins |
Cook: 25 mins | Makes: 4 – 6

INGREDIENTS:

1 ½ cups plain flour

¾ cup yellow cornmeal

½ cup granulated sugar

1 tbsp baking powder

¼ tsp table salt

2 eggs

1 cup canned creamed corn

½ cup unsalted butter, melted

¾ cups whole milk

4 – 6 tbsp butter cubes for topping

Maple syrup for topping

ACCESSORIES:

8 Inch Round Baking Pan

DIRECTIONS:

1. Without any insert, preheat the Indoor Grill. Select Bake, set the temperature to 350°F, the time to 25 minutes, and press Start/Stop to begin preheating.

2. In a large bowl, mix the flour, cornmeal, sugar, baking powder, and salt. Set the dry mix aside.

3. Crack the eggs into a medium bowl and lightly whisk. Pour in the creamed corn, melted butter, milk, and whisk until well combined. Pour the mixture into the dry mix and combine well.

4. Lightly grease the bottom of an 8-inch round baking pan with cooking spray, pour in the batter, and use a spatula to level the top.

5. Once the Indoor Grill has preheated, open the lid and sit the baking pan on the base, close the lid and cook for 20 minutes.

6. When the baking is complete, open the lid and insert a toothpick into the bread to check for doneness. If still watery, close the lid and bake for another 5 minutes.

7. When ready, remove the baking pan with oven mitts and place on a flat surface for 5 minutes to cool. Run a butter knife around the edges of the pan and slice into 4 or 6 wedges, place on serving plates, top each wedge with a tablespoon of butter and squeeze some maple syrup on top. *Note: if you have a wire rack you can remove the entire pan of cornbread onto it for easier slicing.*

☆☆☆☆☆
Rating

Notes:

----

8. Grilled Eggs in Bell Peppers

Level: Simple/Beginner | Function: Grill | Prep: 8 mins | Preheat: 8 mins |
Cook: 10 mins | Makes: 4

INGREDIENTS:

4 medium mixed bell peppers, halved and deseeded (maintain the heads)

8 medium eggs

Salt and black pepper to taste

½ cup grated cheddar cheese

2 tbsp chopped fresh parsley

DIRECTIONS:

1. Insert the grill grate into the Indoor Grill and close the lid. Select Grill, set the temperature to Max, and the time to 10 minutes. Press Start/Stop to initiate preheating.

2. Lay the peppers flat on a plate, crack an egg into each, season with salt, black pepper, and sprinkle the cheese on top.

3. Once the Indoor Grill has heated, open the lid and carefully place the peppers on the grates. Close the lid and cook for 10 minutes.

4. When ready, transfer the peppers to a plate, garnish with parsley and serve warm.

☆☆☆☆☆
Rating

Notes:

----

9. Grilled Nectarine Tart

Level: Simple/Beginner | Function: Grill | Prep: 10 mins | Preheat: 8 mins |
Cook: 15 mins | Makes: 4

INGREDIENTS:

2 tbsp high smoke point oil for brushing

1 (9-inch) round pie dough, refrigerated

½ cup granulated sugar

¼ tsp ginger powder

A pinch nutmeg powder

¼ tsp cinnamon powder

2 lb nectarines, pitted and cut into ½ -inch thick slices

1 tsp freshly squeezed lemon juice

DIRECTIONS:

1. Insert the grill grate into the Indoor Grill and close the lid. Select Grill, set the temperature to Max, and the time to 15 minutes. Press Start/Stop to begin preheating.
2. Cut a large round of heavy-duty foil to fit the pie dough about 2-inches longer than the dough and brush with some oil. Unwrap the dough, lay on the foil and evenly brush the top with oil. Crimp the edges of the foil around the dough to form a rim, which will prevent juice from pouring into the grill.
3. In a medium bowl, mix the sugar, ginger powder, nutmeg powder, and cinnamon powder. Pour in the nectarines, lemon juice, and toss in the sugar mix until well-coated. Spread the fruit mixture on the dough while leaving 1-inch space around the edges. Fold this edge over the fruit to cover slightly and to create some crust after cooking.
4. Once the Indoor Grill has preheated, open the lid and carefully lift the foil with dough onto the grates. Close the lid and cook for 15 minutes or until the dough bakes and is golden brown.
5. When ready, remove the tart with foil onto a flat surface and cool for 2 to 3 minutes.
6. Slice and serve afterwards.

☆☆☆☆☆
Rating

Notes:

----

10. Mushroom and Scallion Omelette

Level: Simple/Beginner | Function: Bake | Prep: 5 mins | Preheat: 3 mins |
Cook: 10 mins | Makes: 4

INGREDIENTS:

8 large eggs

1 cup canned sliced mushrooms, drained

2 scallions, thinly sliced

Salt and black pepper to taste

¼ cup grated brie cheese

DIRECTIONS:

1. Insert the cooking pot into the Indoor Grill and close the lid. Select Bake, set the temperature to 320 F, and the time to 10 minutes. Press Start/Stop to initiate preheating.

2. Crack the eggs into a medium bowl and whisk well. Mix in the mushrooms, scallions, and season with salt and black pepper.

3. Once the Indoor Grill has preheated, pour the egg mix into the cooking pot, spread out with a spatula and sprinkle the brie cheese on top. Close the lid and cook for 10 minutes.

4. Once ready, using oven mitts, remove the pot and empty the omelet onto a plate.

5. Slice and serve immediately.

☆☆☆☆☆
Rating

Notes:

Chicken

Don't be fooled. It is an absolute art to achieve the perfect balance between crispy outside and juicy inside when preparing dishes with chicken. Forgo the misery of serving up an overly dry mess at dinner, and employ your newest Indoor Grill to get you that perfectly cooked chicken every time! For the best results, use these recipes complete with aromatic spices and savory marinades to take your meals to the next level.

It's important to note that chicken must be cooked to an internal temperature of 165F. If you don't happen to have a probe thermometer just laying around, don't fret! A good indication of whether or not your chicken is safe to consume is found in the color of the juices. Clear means you're in the clear while pink indicates additional cooking time is needed.

11. Soy Honey Chicken Breasts with Ginger Hints

Level: Simple/Beginner | Function: Grill | Prep: 10 mins + marinating |
Preheat: 8 mins | Cook: 28 mins | Makes: 4

INGREDIENTS:

1/3 cup light soy sauce

¼ cup honey

1 tbsp fresh ginger paste

4 garlic cloves, minced

½ tsp ground black pepper

4 large chicken breasts, skinless and boneless

2 scallions, chopped for garnishing

DIRECTIONS:

1. In a large, plastic zipper bag, mix the soy sauce, honey, ginger paste, garlic, and black pepper. Add the chicken, zip up the bag, and massage the marinade onto the chicken until well-coated. Put the bag in the fridge (for unfrozen chicken) and freezer (for frozen chicken) and marinate preferably overnight or at least a couple of hours before cooking.

2. When ready to cook, which can be done normal or frozen:

3. For normal temperature:

4. Insert the grill grate into the Indoor Grill and close the lid. Select Grill, set the temperature to Medium, and the time to 18 minutes. Press Start/Stop to initiate preheating.

5. Once the Indoor Grill beeps to have preheated, remove the chicken breasts from the fridge, the bag, and arrange on the grill grate. Close the top and cook for 18 minutes, flipping halfway until the chicken reaches an internal temperature of 165°F when using a meat thermometer.

6. For frozen:

7. Insert the grill grate into the Indoor Grill and close the lid. Select Grill, set the temperature to Medium, and the time to 25 minutes. Press Start/Stop to initiate preheating.

8. Once the Indoor Grill beeps to have preheated, remove the chicken breasts from the freezer, the bag, and arrange on the grill grate. Close the top and cook for 10 minutes. Flip the chicken after 10 minutes, close the lid and cook for 10 more minutes until it cooks to an internal temperature of 165°F.

9. Transfer the chicken to a serving platter to rest (continue self-cook) for 5 minutes.

10. Garnish the chicken with the scallions and serve afterward with your preferred side dish from the category below.

☆☆☆☆☆
Rating

Notes:

----

12. Teriyaki Chicken with Assorted Veggies

Level: Simple/Beginner | Function: Grill | Prep: 15 mins + 2 hours marinating |
Preheat: 8 mins | Cook: 37 mins | Makes: 4

INGREDIENTS:

For the teriyaki chicken:

4 frozen or thawed chicken thighs, bone-in

½ cup mirin

½ cup sake

½ cup soy sauce

¼ cup granulated sugar

2 tbsp fresh ginger paste

1 tbsp onion powder

2 garlic cloves, peeled and crushed

1 tbsp cornstarch

1 tbsp water

For the assorted veggies:

2 large carrots, peeled and diagonally sliced

1 large yellow bell pepper, deseeded and cut into quarters

1 small head broccoli, cut into florets

1 medium yellow onion, peeled and cut into wedges

Salt and black pepper to taste

2 tbsp chopped fresh scallions for garnish

1 tbsp toasted sesame seeds for garnish

DIRECTIONS:

For the teriyaki chicken:

1. Put the chicken in a large zipper bag. In a medium bowl, mix the mirin, sake, soy sauce, sugar, ginger paste, onion powder, garlic, cornstarch, and water. Pour the mixture all over the chicken, seal the bag, and massage the marinade well onto the chicken. Marinate the chicken in the fridge (for thawed chicken) for 2 hours and in the freezer (for frozen) for 3 hours.

When ready to cook, for thawed chicken:

2. Insert the grill grate into the Indoor Grill and close the lid. Select Grill, set the temperature to High, and the time to 18 minutes. Press Start/Stop to begin preheating.

3. Once the Indoor Grill is preheated, remove the chicken from the fridge, the bag, and arrange on the grill grate. Close the top and cook for 18 minutes, flipping halfway until the chicken reaches an internal temperature of 165°F when using a meat thermometer.

For frozen:

4. Insert the grill grate into the Indoor Grill and close the lid. Select Grill, set the temperature to Medium, and the time to 25 minutes. Press Start/Stop to begin preheating.

5. Once the Indoor Grill is preheated, remove the chicken from the freezer, the bag, and arrange on the grill grate. Close the top and cook for 10 minutes. Flip the chicken after 10 minutes, close the lid and cook for 10 to 15 more minutes or until it cooks to an internal temperature of 165°F.

5. When ready, open the lid and transfer the chicken to a plate to rest for 3 minutes.

For the assorted veggies:

6. Meanwhile, in a medium bowl, season the carrots, bell pepper, broccoli, and onion with salt and black pepper. Arrange the vegetables on the grate and close the lid. Change the temperature to Max and set the time to 12 minutes. Cook for 10 minutes, check the desired doneness and cook further for 2 minutes if not done to your likeness.

7. Transfer the vegetables to 4 serving plates, place a chicken thigh on each plate, and garnish the chicken with the scallions and sesame seeds.

8. Serve warm with steamed rice.

☆☆☆☆☆
Rating

Notes:

----

13. Herby Lemon-Garlic Tenders

Level: Simple/Beginner | Function: Grill | Prep: 10 mins + 2 hours marinating |
Preheat: 8 mins | Cook: 10 mins | Makes: 4

INGREDIENTS:

1 ½ lb chicken tenders

6 tbsp high smoke point oil

1 tsp dried thyme

4 garlic cloves, minced

Kosher salt and black pepper to taste

½ tsp dried oregano

1 lemon, zested and juiced

1 tbsp chopped fresh cilantro to garnish

Lemon wedges for serving

DIRECTIONS:

1. Wrap the tenders in plastic and using a meat tenderizer, gently pound the meat into ½-inch thickness. Unwrap the chicken and put in a large zipper bag.

2. In a small bowl, mix the oil, thyme. Garlic, salt, black pepper, oregano, lemon zest, and lemon juice. Pour the mixture over the chicken, seal the bag, and massage the marinade well on the chicken. Place the bag in the refrigerator and marinate for 1 to 2 hours.

When ready to cook:

3. Insert the grill grate into the Indoor Grill and close the lid. Select Grill, set the temperature to High, and the time to 10 minutes. Press Start/Stop to initiate preheating.

4. Remove the bag from the fridge and arrange the chicken tenders on the grate. Close the lid and cook for 10 minutes, flipping halfway.

5. At 8 minutes, check the chicken for doneness; otherwise, cook further until 10 minutes is up.

6. Open the lid and remove the chicken onto a plate to self-cook for 2 to 3 minutes.

7. Plate the chicken, garnish with the cilantro, lemon wedges and serve warm with lettuce and egg salad.

☆☆☆☆☆
Rating

Notes:

----

14. Parmesan-Breaded Chicken Nuggets

Level: Simple/Beginner | Function: Air Crisp | Prep: 10 mins | Preheat: 3 mins |
Cook: 10 mins | Makes: 4

INGREDIENTS:

4 chicken breasts, skinless and boneless, cut into bite-size pieces

Sea salt and black pepper to taste

½ cup finely grated Parmesan cheese

1 cup panko breadcrumbs

½ tsp dried thyme

½ cup plain flour

2 large eggs

High smoke point oil for spraying

For the BBQ mustard dipping sauce (or use any premade sauce you love):

½ cup mayonnaise

2 tbsp BBQ sauce

1 tbsp Dijon mustard

1 tbsp yellow mustard

2 ½ tbsp honey

DIRECTIONS:

1. Insert the crisper basket into the Indoor Grill and close the lid. Select Air Crisp, set the temperature to 375°F, the time to 30 minutes, and press Start/Stop to initiate preheating.

2. On a wide plate, mix the Parmesan cheese, breadcrumbs, and thyme. On another plate, pour the flour. Crack the eggs into a small bowl and lightly whisk.

3. Generously season the chicken with salt and black pepper. Dredge the chicken lightly in the flour, then in the eggs, and then generously coat in the breadcrumbs mixture.

4. Once the Indoor Grill has preheated, arrange the coated chicken in the basket, spray with some oil, and close the lid. Cook for 25 minutes, shaking the basket halfway. Check doneness at 20 minutes; cook 5 more minutes if needed.

5. Transfer the chicken nuggets to a serving plate, allow cooling for 2 minutes and serve warm with the dipping sauce. For the dipping sauce:

6. While the chicken is cooking, mix the mayonnaise, BBQ sauce, Dijon mustard, yellow mustard, and honey in a small bowl using a fork or small whisk until combined and smooth.

☆☆☆☆☆
Rating

Notes:

----

15. Garlic-Herb-Butter Spatchcock Chicken

Level: Mid | Function: Grill | Prep: 15 mins | Preheat: 8 mins |
Cook: 60 mins | Makes: 4

INGREDIENTS:

1 whole chicken (3 lb)

3 tbsp high smoke point oil

¼ cup unsalted butter, melted

1 lemon, halved

4 garlic cloves, minced

2 tbsp chopped fresh parsley

Kosher salt and black pepper to taste

3 fresh rosemary sprigs

DIRECTIONS:

1. Insert the grill grate into the Indoor Grill and close the lid. Select Grill, set the temperature to High, the time to 60 minutes, and press Start/Stop to initiate preheating.

2. Place the chicken on a chopping board and using sharp kitchen shears, cut around the backbone from neck to tail. Remove the backbone and turn the chicken over to the breast side. Carefully split the back apart and gently press down the breast until the chicken lays flat on the board (a ¼ inch cut along the cartilage above the breast bone makes this process easier). Move the wing tips behind the back and adjust the legs to be symmetrical. Using paper towels, pat the skin dry.

3. In a small bowl, mix the oil, butter, lemon juice, garlic, parsley, salt, and black pepper. Brush all parts of the chicken with the mixture.

4. Once the grill has preheated, open the lid and lay the chicken on the grates (with breast side up). Place the rosemary sprigs on top, close the lid, and cook for 50 minutes (flipping after 30 minutes). Check the chicken's doneness (165F in the thickest part of the breast if using a probe thermometer) and cook further for 10 minutes if not done or until the thermometer reads 165F.

5. When ready, using tongs, transfer the chicken to a cleaned chopping board (discard the rosemary), allow chicken to rest for 5 to 8 minutes before slicing and serving.

☆☆☆☆☆
Rating

Notes:

----

16. Hawaiian Style Fried Chicken

Level: Simple/Beginner | Function: Air Crisp | Prep: 10 mins | Preheat: 3 mins |
Cook: 20 mins | Makes: 4

INGREDIENTS:

4 chicken thighs, skinless and boneless

1 tsp kosher salt

3 medium eggs

¼ cup water

¼ cup cornstarch

3 cups panko breadcrumbs

High smoke point oil for spraying

DIRECTIONS:

1. Insert the crisper basket into the Indoor Grill and close the lid. Select Air Crisp, set the temperature to 390°F, the time to 20 minutes, and press Start/Stop to initiate preheating.

2. Pat the chicken pieces dry with a paper towel and season well with ½ tsp of salt.

3. Crack the eggs into a shallow plate and whisk with the water, cornstarch, and remaining salt. Pour the breadcrumbs into a flat plate.

4. Coat each chicken on all sides in the egg mixture and then generously in the breadcrumbs.

5. Once the Indoor Grill has preheated, lightly spray the crisper basket with some oil, lay the chicken in the basket, and spray the tops with oil. Close the lid and cook for 20 minutes, flipping halfway.

6. After 20 minutes (or until 165F internal temperature), transfer the chicken to a plate and allow to rest for 2 to 3 minutes.

7. Serve the chicken pieces warm with coleslaw, rice, or French fries.

☆☆☆☆☆
Rating

Notes:

----

17. Smoky & Sweet Cider Drumsticks

Level: Simple/Beginner | Function: Grill | Prep: 10 mins + 6 hours marinating |
Preheat: 8 mins | Cook: 14 mins | Makes: 4

INGREDIENTS:

4 (7 oz) chicken drumsticks

1 tbsp high smoke point oil

1 tbsp apple cider vinegar

1 tbsp yellow mustard

1 tsp liquid smoke

1 tbsp Worcestershire sauce

1 tbsp ketchup

½ tbsp soy sauce

½ tbsp brown sugar

1 tbsp chopped fresh scallions for garnishing

DIRECTIONS:

1. Put the chicken pieces in a large zipper bag. In a small bowl, mix the oil, apple cider vinegar, yellow mustard, liquid smoke, Worcestershire sauce, ketchup, soy sauce, and brown sugar until the sugar dissolves. Pour the mixture over the chicken, zip up the bag, and massage the marinade onto the drumettes until well coated. Place in the refrigerator to marinate for 6 hours or overnight.

2. When ready to cook, insert the grill grate into the Indoor Grill and close the lid. Select Grill, set the temperature to High, the time to 14 minutes, and press Start/Stop to initiate preheating.

3. Once the Indoor Grill has preheated, remove the chicken from the bag and arrange on the grill grate. Close the lid and cook for 14 minutes. After 7 minutes, open the lid and brush the top of the chicken with some of the marinade. Flip the pieces, brush with more marinade, and close the lid. Cook until the timer ends or until the internal temperature reads 165°F.

4. Once ready, transfer the chicken to a serving platter and allow resting for 3 to 5 minutes.

5. Garnish the chicken with scallions and serve warm.

☆☆☆☆☆
Rating

Notes:

----

18. Greek Chicken Kebab

Level: Simple/Beginner | Function: Grill | Prep: 15 mins + overnight marinating |
Preheat: 8 mins | Cook: 14 mins | Makes: 4

INGREDIENTS:

4 chicken breasts, cut into 1-inch cubes

1 lemon, zested and juiced

¼ cup olive oil

6 garlic cloves, minced

1 tsp kosher salt

½ tsp black pepper

2 tbsp chopped fresh oregano

2 tbsp chopped fresh parsley

1 small zucchini, sliced into coins

1 medium red onion, quartered

1 medium red bell pepper, deseeded and cut into large cubes

DIRECTIONS:

1. Pour the chicken into a large zipper bag. In a small bowl, mix the lemon zest, lemon juice, garlic, salt, black pepper, oregano, and parsley. Pour the mixture over the chicken, zip up the bag, and massage the marinade onto the chicken onto well coated. Place the bag in the refrigerator and allow the chicken marinate overnight.

2. When ready to cook, insert the grill grate into the Indoor Grill and close the lid. Select Grill, set the temperature to High, the time to 14 minutes, and press Start/Stop to initiate preheating.

3. While the Indoor Grill preheats, remove the chicken from the fridge and alternately thread on 4 skewers with the zucchini, onion, and bell pepper.

4. Once the Indoor Grill has preheated, open the lid and lay the skewers on the grate. Close the lid and cook for 14 minutes, flipping halfway.

5. Transfer the kebab to serving plates when ready and serve warm with Greek salad.

☆☆☆☆☆
Rating

Notes:

----

19. Old Bay Buffalo Wings

Level: Simple/Beginner | Function: Grill | Prep: 5 mins | Preheat: 8 mins |
Cook: 14 mins | Makes: 6 – 8

INGREDIENTS:

¼ cup plain flour

2 tbsp dried Old Bay seasoning

2 lb chicken wings, bone-in

¼ cup buffalo hot sauce

¼ cup melted butter

1 cup crumbled blue cheese for topping

Celery sticks for serving

DIRECTIONS:

1. Insert the grill grate into the Indoor Grill and close the lid. Select Grill, set the temperature to High, the time to 14 minutes, and press Start/Stop to initiate preheating.

2. Pour the flour and Old Bay seasoning into a large zipper bag. Close the bag and vigorously shake until both ingredients mix well.

3. Season the chicken well with salt, add to the flour in the bag, close the bag again and shake well until the chicken is well-coated with the flour mix.

4. Once the Indoor Grill has preheated, open the lid and arrange the chicken on the grate in a single layer. Close the lid and cook for 14 minutes, flipping halfway.

5. Meanwhile, in a large bowl, mix the buffalo sauce and butter. Transfer the chicken to the bowl when ready and toss in the sauce until well-coated.

6. Dish the chicken, top with the blue cheese and serve warm with the celery sticks.

☆☆☆☆☆
Rating

Notes:

----

20. Bourbon BBQ Wings

Level: Simple/Beginner | Function: Grill | Prep: 15 mins + marinating |
Preheat: 8 mins | Cook: 14 mins | Makes: 4

INGREDIENTS:

½ cup bourbon

2 tbsp favorite chicken rub

2 tbsp high smoke point oil

1 tsp garlic powder

1 tsp onion powder

2 cups ketchup

½ cup brown sugar

¼ cup Worcestershire sauce

1 lemon, juiced

1 tsp kosher salt (if needed)

½ tsp black pepper

2 lb chicken wings

1 tbsp chopped fresh scallions for garnishing

DIRECTIONS:

1. In a large bowl, mix the bourbon, chicken seasoning, oil, garlic powder, onion powder, ketchup, brown sugar, worcestershire sauce, salt (if needed), and black pepper. Add the chicken wings, mix well and cover the bowl with plastic wrap. Place the bowl in the refrigerator and marinate for 1 hour.

2. After 1 hour, insert the grill grate into the Indoor Grill and close the lid. Select Grill, set the temperature to High, the time to 14 minutes, and press Start/Stop to initiate preheating. Also, remove the chicken from the fridge.

3. Once the Indoor Grill has preheated, remove the chicken from the marinade, and arrange the on the grate in a single layer (discard the marinade). Close the lid and cook for 14 minutes, flipping halfway. If all the wings do not fit, cook in batches.

4. When the chicken is ready, transfer the pieces to a plate to self-cook for 3 to 5 more minutes.

5. Plate the chicken, garnish with the scallions and serve warm.

☆☆☆☆☆
Rating

Notes:

Beef

Nothing quite creates the perfect evening like a nicely cooked steak. But nothing will quite ruin the evening like an overly charred steak that even the best steak knife struggles to get through. The key to a steak that melts like butter in the mouth is a gentle sear on the outside while achieving the internal doneness that most suits your taste. Keep in mind that cooking times for steaks vary according to the cut and thickness so the times here are general guidelines. To more accurately check doneness, use a probe thermometer and reference the temperature chart below.

Beef Internal Temperature Chart

Rare	(cool red center)	115°F – 125°F
Medium Rare	(warm red center)	120°F – 125°F
Medium	(warm pink center)	130°F – 135°F
Medium Well	(slightly pink center)	140°F – 145°F
Well done	(little or no pink)	150°F – 155°F

21. Parsley Buttered Ribeye with Green Beans

Level: Simple / Beginner | Function: Grill | Prep: 10 mins | Preheat: 8 mins |
Cook: 12 to 14 mins | Makes: 2

INGREDIENTS:

2 bone-in ribeye steaks, 1 ¼ -inch thick

2 tsp kosher salt

2 to 3 tbsp high smoke point oil for brushing

1 tsp black peppercorns, coarsely ground

2 tbsp salted butter for topping

1 tbsp chopped fresh parsley for garnishing

1 ½ to 2 cups green beans, trimmed

DIRECTIONS:

1. Pat dry the steak with paper towels, place on a clean, flat surface, brush the oil on both sides of the steak and season the meat with ¼ tsp each of salt and black peppercorns per side, and press the seasoning onto the beef to adhere.

2. Insert the grill grate into the Indoor Grill and close the lid. Select Grill, set the temperature to High, and set the time to 8-10 minutes, depending on how you like your steak. Press Start/Stop to begin preheating.

3. Once preheated, place the steaks on the grill grate while gently pressing for grill marks during cooking. Close the lid and cook, flipping halfway. 8 minutes total time should bring the steak to Medium doneness. Adjust the time lower or higher depending on your preference

4. When the steak is ready to your preferred doneness, transfer to two serving plates, top with the butter, garnish with the parsley, and allow to rest for 5 minutes.

6. Meanwhile, arrange the green beans on the grill grate. Close the lid, select Grill, set the temperature to High, and the time to 4 minutes. Select Start/Stop to begin cooking while the beef sits.

7. When ready, using tongs, place the green beans around or to the side of the steaks (whole or sliced), and serve immediately.

☆☆☆☆☆
Rating

Notes:

----

22. Lemon Pepper Filet Mignon

Level: Simple / Beginner | Function: Grill | Prep: 10 mins | Preheat: 8 mins |
Cook: 12 to 14 mins | Makes: 4

INGREDIENTS:

4 filet mignon steaks

4 tbsp high smoke point oil

Kosher salt to taste

1/3 cup whole peppercorns, mixed colors and crushed

1 lemon, juiced

DIRECTIONS:

1. Insert the grill grate into the Indoor Grill and close the lid. Select Grill, set the temperature to High, and set the time to 14 minutes. Press Start/Stop to initiate preheating.

2. Pat dry the steaks using a paper towel, brush the oil on both sides of the meat and season well with salt and peppercorns.

3. Once the Indoor Grill, has preheated, open the lid and arrange the meat on the grate. Close the lid and cook for 12-15 minutes, depending on how you like your steak, flipping halfway.

4. When ready to your preferred doneness, transfer the meat to a clean chopping board and allow resting for 5 minutes.

5. Drizzle a little lemon juice on the meat and serve warm.

☆☆☆☆☆
Rating

Notes:

----

23. Rosemary Butter T-Bone Steak

Level: Simple / Beginner | Function: Grill | Prep: 10 mins | Preheat: 8 mins |
Cook: 9 to 12 mins | Makes: 4

INGREDIENTS:

1 ½ lb T-bone steak, 1-inch thick

2 tbsp high smoke point oil

Kosher salt and black pepper to taste

4 fresh rosemary sprigs

2 tbsp unsalted butter for topping

DIRECTIONS:

1. Insert the grill grate into the Indoor Grill and close the lid. Select Grill, set the temperature to High, and set the time to 12 minutes. Press Start/Stop to initiate preheating.

2. Pat dry the steak using paper towels and rub well on both sides with the oil. Season liberally with salt and black pepper.

3. Once the Indoor Grill has preheated, open the lid, lay the steak on the grate, and spread the rosemary sprigs on the meat. Close the lid and cook for 9-12 minutes depending on how you like your steak, flipping halfway.

4. Once ready to your desired doneness, transfer the meat to a clean cutting surface and let it rest for 5 minutes.

5. Place the butter on the meat while still hot to melt onto the meat and then slice afterward.

6. Serve warm.

Rating

Notes:

----

24. Flat-Iron Steak with Balsamic Tomato Relish

Level: Simple / Beginner | Function: Grill | Prep: 15 mins + 30 mins marinating |
Preheat: 8 mins | Cook: 12 to 15 mins | Makes: 4

INGREDIENTS:

For the steak:

4 (8 oz) flat-iron steak

2 tbsp high smoke point oil for brushing

Kosher salt and black pepper to taste

For the roasted tomato relish:

3 large firm, ripe tomatoes, cut into quarters

1 large onion, cut into wedges

2 tsp high smoke point oil for coating

Sea salt and black pepper to taste

2 tbsp balsamic vinegar

2 garlic cloves, minced

½ tsp red chili flakes

¼ cup chopped fresh chives

¼ cup chopped fresh parsley

4 tbsp olive oil for drizzling

DIRECTIONS:

For the steak:

1. Insert the grill grate into the Indoor Grill and close the lid. Select Grill, set the temperature to High, and set the time to 10 minutes. Press Start/Stop to initiate preheating.

2. Pat dry the steak using paper towels, brush both sides of each steak with oil, and season well with salt and black pepper. Allow sitting for 20 to 30 minutes to marinate.

3. Once the Indoor Grill has preheated, open the lid, and lay the steak pieces on the grate. Close the lid and cook for 7-10 minutes depending how you like your steak, flipping halfway.

4. Once ready to your desired doneness, transfer the meat to a platter and allow sitting to self-cook for 5 more minutes.

Meanwhile, prepare the balsamic tomato relish:

5. In a medium bowl, add the tomatoes, onion, oil, salt, black pepper, and toss until the vegetables are well coated.

6. With the grill grate still on the Indoor Grill, reset the Indoor Grill temperature to Max, and the time to 5 minutes.

7. Arrange the tomatoes and onion pieces on the grate in a single layer, close the lid, and press Start/Stop to cook the vegetables.

8. After 5 minutes, using tongs, transfer the vegetables to a chopping board and cut into small pieces. Put the mixture in a bowl and mix well with the balsamic vinegar, garlic, red chili flakes, chives, and parsley. Drizzle with some olive oil afterwards.

9. Serve the flank steak warm with the tomato relish.

☆☆☆☆☆
Rating

Notes:

----

25. Churrasco with Spicy Chimichurri and Cherry Tomato Salad

Level: Simple / Beginner | Function: Grill | Prep: 20 mins + 30 mins marinating |
Preheat: 9 mins | Cook: 12 to 15 mins | Makes: 4

INGREDIENTS:

For the chimichurri:

2 cups fresh curly parsley, thick stems removed

4 garlic cloves, crushed

1 long red chili, head removed

3 tbsp white wine vinegar

¾ cup olive oil

Sea salt to taste

For the cherry tomato salad:

2 cups mixed colored cherry tomatoes, halved

1 tsp red wine vinegar

Sea salt and black pepper to taste

¼ tsp dried oregano

2 oz crumbled feta cheese

1 tbsp olive oil

For the churrasco:

2 lb skirt steak

Kosher salt and black pepper to taste

DIRECTIONS:

For the chimichurri:

1. In a food processor, add the parsley, garlic, red chili, white wine vinegar, ¼ cup of olive oil, and salt. Pulse a few times until the ingredients are coarsely combined. Pour the mixture into a bowl and mix in the remaining olive oil. Set the chimichurri aside to allow the flavors to combine.

For the cherry tomato salad:

2. In a large bowl, mix the tomatoes, vinegar, salt, black pepper, oregano, feta cheese, and olive oil. Set aside to allow the flavors to combine.

For the churrasco:

3. Insert the grill grate into the Indoor Grill and close the lid. Select Grill, set the temperature to High, and set the time to 7-9 minutes, depending on how you like your steak. Press Start/Stop to initiate preheating.

4. Pat dry the steak using paper towels, brush some high smoke point oil and generously season both sides with the salt and black pepper. Cut into pieces if it is too large to fit on the grill surface.

5. Once the Indoor Grill has preheated, open the lid and lay the steak pieces on the grate. Close the lid and cook for 7-9 minutes, depending on how you like your steak, flipping halfway.

6. Once cooked to your desired doneness, transfer the meat to a chopping board and let sit for 5 minutes to rest.

7. After resting the steak, slice the churrasco with the knife at a 45 degree angle and arrange on a serving platter. Spoon 3 to 4 tablespoons of the chimichurri over the meat and serve warm with the tomato salad.

☆☆☆☆☆
Rating

Notes:

----

26. Sesame Sirloin Steak

Level: Simple / Beginner | Function: Grill | Prep: 15 mins + 30 mins marinating |
Preheat: 8 mins | Cook: 12 to 15 mins | Makes: 4

INGREDIENTS:

2 lb beef sirloin steak

½ cup high smoke point oil for brushing

Kosher salt and black pepper to taste

2 tbsp toasted sesame seeds for garnish

DIRECTIONS:

1. Insert the grill grate into the Indoor Grill and close the lid. Select Grill, set the temperature to High, and set the time to 7-9 minutes, depending on how you like your steak. Press Start/Stop to initiate preheating.

2. Pat the meat dry with paper towels, brush both sides of the beef with oil, and season well with salt and black pepper. Cut into pieces if it will not fit on the grill surface.

3. Once the Indoor Grill has preheated, open the lid and place the meat on the grate. Close the lid and cook for 7-9 minutes, depending on how you like your steak, flipping halfway.

4. When the meat cooks to your desired doneness, transfer to a chopping board and let it rest for 5 minutes.

5. After, slice the meat with the knife at a 45 degree angle, sprinkle the sesame seeds on top and serve warm with mashed potatoes and mushrooms sauce.

☆☆☆☆☆
Rating

Notes:

----

27. Grilled Hanger Steak with Mushroom Gravy

Level: Simple / Beginner | Function: Grill | Prep: 15 mins + 30 mins marinating | Preheat: 8 mins | Cook: 12 to 15 mins | Makes: 4

INGREDIENTS:

For the steak:

1 ½ lb hanger steak

Kosher salt and black pepper to taste

For the mushroom gravy:

1 (28 oz) can sliced mushrooms, drained

¼ cup yellow onion, chopped

2 tbsp olive oil

2 tsp heavy cream

2 tsp soy sauce

½ tsp dried thyme

1 tbsp dried parsley

Black pepper to taste

½ cup water

DIRECTIONS:

1. Insert the grill grate into the Indoor Grill and close the lid. Select Grill, set the temperature to High, and set the time to 7-10 minutes, depending on how you like your steak. Press Start/Stop to initiate preheating.
2. Pat the beef dry with paper towels and season generously with salt and black pepper.
3. Once the Indoor Grill has preheated, open the lid and place the beef on the grate. Close the lid and cook for 15 minutes, depending on how you like your steak, flipping halfway.
4. When cooked to your desired doneness, transfer the steak to a chopping board and let it rest for 5 minutes before slicing.

For the mushroom sauce:

5. Meanwhile, as the steak rests, in a food processor, add the mushrooms, onion, olive oil, heavy cream, soy sauce, thyme, parsley, and black pepper. Blend on medium speed until smooth.
6. Pour the gravy into a sauce cup and serve along with the meat.

☆☆☆☆☆
Rating

Notes:

----

28. Classic Coffee-Rubbed Ribeye Steak

Level: Simple / Beginner | Function: Grill | Prep: 15 mins | Preheat: 8 mins | Cook: 8 to 10 mins | Makes: 2

INGREDIENTS:

½ tbsp finely ground coffee

½ tbsp kosher salt

½ tbsp black pepper

½ tbsp brown sugar

½ tbsp mustard powder

½ tbsp paprika

½ tbsp red chili flakes

½ tbsp garlic granules

2 boneless rib-eye steaks

DIRECTIONS:

1. Insert the grill grate into the Indoor Grill and close the lid. Select Grill, set the temperature to High, and set the time to 8-10 minutes, depending on how you like your steak. Press Start/Stop to initiate preheating.

2. In a medium bowl, mix the coffee, salt, black pepper, brown sugar, mustard powder, paprika, red chili flakes, and garlic granules. Pat the meat dry and spread the dry rub on all sides of the meat making sure to press the seasoning onto the meat to adhere.

3. Once the Indoor Grill has preheated, open the lid and place the steaks on top. Close the lid and cook for 8-10 minutes, depending on how you like your steak, flipping halfway.

4. When the steaks are done, transfer to a chopping board and let them rest for 5 minutes.

5. Serve right after the 5 minutes are up.

☆☆☆☆☆
Rating

Notes:

----

29. Ginger-Lemongrass Short Ribs

Level: Simple / Beginner | Function: Grill | Prep: 15 mins + 30 mins marinating |
Preheat: 8 mins | Cook: 20 mins | Makes: 4

INGREDIENTS:

3 tbsp soy sauce

1 large lime, juiced

2 stalks fresh lemongrass, minced

1 tbsp fresh ginger paste

3 garlic cloves, minced

2 tbsp fish sauce

2 tbsp avocado oil

2 tsp sesame oil

4 tbsp brown sugar

2 lb short ribs, cut into individual ribs

1 tbsp chopped fresh scallions for garnish

1 tbsp toasted sesame seeds for garnish

DIRECTIONS:

1. In a small bowl, mix the soy sauce, lime juice, lemongrass, ginger, garlic, fish sauce, avocado oil, sesame oil, and brown sugar. Pat the ribs dry with paper towels and brush all sides except the bones with the marinade mix. Cover the beef with plastic wrap and marinate in the refrigerator for 6 hours.

2. Remove the meat 30 minutes prior to cooking to return to room temperature.

3. After 20 minutes, insert the grill grate into the Indoor Grill and close the lid. Select Grill, set the temperature to High, and set the time to 20 minutes. Press Start/Stop to initiate preheating.

4. Once preheated, open the lid, and place the rib pieces on the grate. Close the lid and cook for 15-20 minutes, flipping halfway. Be careful not to overcook or they will come out tough!

5. When cooked to your desired doneness, remove the ribs onto a chopping board and allow to rest for 5 minutes.

6. Slice the ribs, garnish with the scallions, sesame seeds, and serve warm.

☆☆☆☆☆
Rating

Notes:

----

30. Yogurt Marinated Steak Tips

Level: Simple / Beginner | Function: Grill | Prep: 15 mins + 30 mins marinating |
Preheat: 8 mins | Cook: 6-10 mins | Makes: 4

INGREDIENTS:

2 lb sirloin steak tips, cut into 2 to 3-inch pieces

½ cup whole-fat yogurt

1 tsp garlic powder

1 tsp onion powder

1 tbsp kosher salt

½ tsp black pepper

DIRECTIONS:

1. Pour the meat into a large zipper bag. In a small bowl, mix the yogurt, garlic powder, onion powder, salt, and black pepper. Pour the mixture on the meat, seal the bag and using your hands, massage the marinade onto the meat until well coated. Place the bag in the refrigerator to marinate the meat for 6 hours.

2. 30 minutes before cooking, remove the bag and allow it to return to room temperature.

3. After 20 minutes, insert the grill grate into the Indoor Grill and close the lid. Select Grill, set the temperature to High, and set the time to 6-10 minutes, depending on how you like your steak. Press Start/Stop to initiate preheating.

4. Once preheated, open the lid, and arrange the meat on the grate. Close the lid and cook, flipping halfway.

5. When the meat is ready to your desired doneness, transfer to a serving platter and allow sitting for 5 minutes before serving.

☆☆☆☆☆
Rating

Notes:

Pork, Lamb & Veal

Pork, lamb, and veal dishes while more rarely incorporated into the weekly menu, are tried and true delicacies with ample versatility. The secret to crafting the most appetizing dish is really no secret at all. It is all about finding the best combination of spice rubs for flavor and marinades to get the tastiest cut every time.

Similar to other meat dishes, internal temperature is important. While visual cues are useful, the best way to verify internal temperatures is a probe thermometer. Reference the chart below to ensure you're serving a fully-cooked meal.

Pork Type & Temp. Requirement

Ground Pork	160°F
Pre-cooked Ham	140°F
Pork Belly	Tender
Ribs	Tender
Pork Shoulder	Tender
Cutlets	Tender
Roasts	145°F to 160°F
Pork chops	145°F to 160°F
Pork Tenderloin	145°F to 160°F

Doneness Temp. Range

Medium Rare	145°F to 150°F
Medium	150°F to 155°F
Medium Well	155°F to 160°F
Well done	160°F

Lamb & Veal Temp. Requirement

Rare	115°F to 120°F
Medium Rare	120°F to 125°F
Medium	130°F to 135°F
Medium Well	140°F to 145°F
Well done	150°F to 155°F
Ground	– 160°F

31. Mustard-Paprika Rubbed Pork Chops

Level: Simple / Beginner | Function: Grill | Prep: 10 mins | Preheat: 8 mins |
Cook: 12 to 14 mins (fresh) __20 to 23 mins (frozen) | Makes: 4

INGREDIENTS:

2 ½ tsp mustard powder

1 tsp paprika

2 tbsp brown sugar

2 tsp kosher salt

1 tsp black pepper

½ tsp cayenne pepper

4 pork chops, boneless (fresh or frozen)

DIRECTIONS:

1. In a small bowl, mix the mustard powder, paprika, brown sugar, salt, black pepper, and cayenne pepper.

For fresh chops:

2. Insert the grill grate into the Indoor Grill and close the lid. Select Grill, set the temperature to High, and set the time to 14 minutes. Press Start/Stop to initiate preheating.

3. Pat dry the chops on both sides with a paper towel and generously spread the rub on all sides of the meat. Press the rub onto the meat to adhere well.

4. Once the Indoor Grill has preheated, open the lid and lay the pork pieces on top. Close the lid and cook for 12 minutes, flipping two to three times. Use a meat thermometer (or if using the probe) to check for your preferred doneness. Cook further for a minute or two if needed.

5. When ready, transfer the chops to a flat plate to rest for 3 minutes before serving.

For frozen chops:

6. Insert the grill grate into the Indoor Grill and close the lid. Select Grill, set the temperature to Medium, and set the time to 20 minutes. Press Start/Stop to initiate preheating.

7. Use paper towels to pat off some of the liquid formed on the meat and then, quickly and generously spread the rub on both sides of the meat.

8. Once the Indoor Grill has preheated, open the lid and lay the pork pieces on top. Close the lid and cook for 20 minutes, flipping two to three times. Use a meat thermometer (or if using the probe) to check for your preferred doneness. Cook further for a minute or two if needed.

9. When ready, transfer the chops to a flat plate to rest for 3 minutes before serving.

☆☆☆☆☆
Rating

Notes:

----

32. Ginger-Orange Grilled Tenderloin

Level: Simple / Beginner | Function: Grill | Prep: 10 mins + 4 to 6 hours marinating|
Preheat: 8 mins | Cook: 15 to 18 mins (fresh)_20 mins (frozen) | Makes: 4 to 6

INGREDIENTS:

1 ½ lb pork tenderloin, cut into 4 pieces

1 orange, juiced

1 tbsp fresh ginger paste

½ cup soy sauce

2 tbsp Dijon mustard

2 tbsp brown sugar

1 tbsp high smoke point oil

Orange quarters for garnishing

DIRECTIONS:

1. Trim the pork of any silverskin or excess fat and place in a large zipper bag.

2. In a small bowl, mix the orange juice, ginger paste, soy sauce, Dijon mustard, brown sugar, and oil.

For fresh tenderloin:

3. Pour the marinade over the pork, seal the bag and massage the seasoning well onto the pork. Place the bag in the refrigerator to marinate for 4 hours.

4. Insert the grill grate into the Indoor Grill and close the lid. Select Grill, set the temperature to High, and set the time to 20 minutes. Press Start/Stop to initiate preheating.

5. Once the Indoor Grill has preheated, open the lid and insert the pork. Close the lid and cook for 15 minutes, flipping two to three times. Use a meat thermometer (or the probe) to check for your preferred doneness. Cook the meat further for 2 to 5 minutes if it is needed.

For frozen tenderloin:

3. Pour the marinade over the pork, seal the bag and massage the seasoning well onto the pork. Place the bag in the freezer to marinate for 4 to 6 hours (or until a later date).

4. Insert the grill grate into the Indoor Grill and close the lid. Select Grill, set the temperature to Medium, and set the time to 20 minutes. Press Start/Stop to initiate preheating.

5. Once the Indoor Grill has preheated, open the lid and place the pork on the grate. Close the lid and cook for 20 minutes, flipping two to three times. Use a meat thermometer (or the probe) to check for your preferred doneness. Cook the meat further for 2 to 5 minutes if it is needed.

6. When ready, transfer the meat to a clean, flat surface and allow resting for 3 minutes.

7. Slice and serve afterward.

☆☆☆☆☆
Rating

Notes:

----

33. Asian BBQ Spareribs

Level: Simple / Beginner | Function: Grill | Prep: 10 mins + overnight marinating|
Preheat: 8 mins | Cook: 20 to 23 mins | Makes: 4

INGREDIENTS:

1 (3 lb) rack pork spareribs, cut into ribs

¼ cup soy sauce

¾ cup brandy

¼ cup hoisin sauce

4 cups honey

½ cup ketchup

1 tbsp kosher salt

½ tsp garlic powder

½ tsp ginger powder

½ tsp Chinese five-spice powder

½ tsp white pepper powder

DIRECTIONS:

1. Place the ribs in a large zipper bag. In a medium bowl, mix the soy sauce, brandy, hoisin sauce, honey, ketchup, salt, garlic powder, ginger powder, Chinese five-spice powder, and white pepper. Pour half of the marinade into the bag and reserve the rest for basting. Seal the bag, massage the marinade well onto the ribs, and place in the refrigerator to marinate overnight.

2. When ready to cook, remove the ribs from the refrigerator onto a plate while the Indoor Grill is preheating. Discard the marinade.

3. Insert the grill grate into the Indoor Grill and close the lid. Select Grill, set the temperature to High, and the time to 20 minutes. Press Start/Stop to initiate preheating.

4. Once the Indoor Grill has preheated, open the lid and working in batches, lay the ribs on the grate. Close the lid and cook for 20 minutes, flipping and basting halfway with the reserved marinade. Use a fork to check the tenderness of the meat, if still firm; cook the ribs for 2 to 3 more minutes.

5. Transfer the ribs to a chopping board when ready and allow to rest for 3 more minutes.

6. Slice the ribs and serve warm.

☆☆☆☆☆
Rating

Notes:

----

34. Herby Cajun Rubbed Baby Back Ribs

Level: Simple / Beginner | Function: Grill | Prep: 5 mins | Preheat: 8 mins |
Cook: 20 to 23 mins | Makes: 4

INGREDIENTS:

½ tsp dry Cajun seasoning ½ tbsp garlic powder

1 tbsp paprika

½ tsp kosher salt

1 tbsp black pepper

½ tsp dried thyme

½ tsp dried basil

¾ tsp onion powder

½ tsp cayenne pepper

¼ cup dark brown sugar

1 (3 lb) rack baby back ribs, cut into individual ribs

DIRECTIONS:

1. Insert the grill grate into the Indoor Grill and close the lid. Select Grill, set the temperature to High, and the time to 20 minutes. Press Start/Stop to initiate preheating.

2. In a small bowl, mix the Cajun seasoning, garlic powder, paprika, salt, black pepper, thyme, basil, powder, onion powder, cayenne pepper, and dark brown sugar.

3. Pat dry the ribs on both sides with paper towels and generously spread, and press the rub on the meat to adhere.

4. Once the Indoor Grill has preheated, open the lid and lay the ribs on the grate. Close the lid and cook for 20 minutes, flipping halfway. Check the meat's tenderness with a fork; otherwise, cook further for 2 to 3 minutes.

5. Transfer the ribs to a chopping board when ready and allow to rest for 3 more minutes.

6. Slice the ribs and serve warm.

☆☆☆☆☆
Rating

Notes:

----

35. Bacon-Wrapped Brussels Sprouts

Level: Simple / Beginner | Function: Grill | Prep: 10 mins + 20 mins marinating|
Preheat: 8 mins | Cook: 15 mins | Makes: 4

INGREDIENTS:

1 tbsp high smoke point oil

¼ tsp garlic powder

¼ tsp black pepper

1/3 cup soy sauce, low sodium

16 Brussels sprouts, halved lengthwise

8 bacon slices, halved

2 to 3 skewers

DIRECTIONS:

1. In a medium bowl, mix the oil, garlic powder, black pepper, and soy sauce. Pour in the Brussels sprouts and fold into the marinade until well-coated. Set aside to marinate for 20 minutes.

2. 12 minutes into the marinating time, insert the grill grate into the Indoor Grill and close the lid. Select Grill, set the temperature to Low, and the time to 15 minutes. Press Start/Stop to initiate preheating.

3. While the Indoor Grill preheats, wrap one Brussels sprout half with a bacon half and insert onto a skewer. Repeat this process until all the Brussels sprouts are wrapped with bacon and the skewers full.

4. Once the Indoor Grill has preheated, open the lid and arrange the skewers on the grate in a single layer. Close the top and cook for 15 minutes, flipping halfway.

5. Transfer the skewers to serving plates and serve warm after.

☆☆☆☆☆
Rating

Notes:

----

36. Fennel & Rosemary Crusted Lamb Rack

Level: Simple / Beginner | Function: Grill | Prep: 10 mins + 4 hours marinating|
Preheat: 8 mins | Cook: 12 to 14 mins | Makes: 4

INGREDIENTS:

1 tbsp fresh rosemary leaves

2 tbsp fennel seeds

3 garlic cloves, minced

1 ½ tbsp kosher salt

1 tbsp black pepper

2 tbsp olive oil

1 lamb rack, 4 ribs

DIRECTIONS:

1. In a small bowl, mix the rosemary, fennel seeds, garlic, salt, black pepper, and olive oil. Trim off excess fat on the lamb, spread and press the seasoning all over the meat to adhere. Wrap the meat in plastic and marinate in the fridge for 4 hours.

2. Insert the grill grate into the Indoor Grill and close the lid. Select Grill, set the temperature to High, and the time to 14 minutes. Press Start/Stop to initiate preheating.

3. Once the Indoor Grill has preheated, open the lid and place the lamb rack on top. Close the lid and cook for 12-14 minutes, flipping halfway. Use a meat thermometer to check for your preferred doneness; otherwise, cook and check temperature at every 2-minute interval until it is the desired internal temperature.

4. When the lamb is ready, transfer to a cutting board and allow to rest for 2 to 3 minutes.

5. Slice and serve afterward.

☆☆☆☆☆
Rating

Notes:

----

37. Greek-Style Grilled Lamb Chops

Level: Simple / Beginner | Function: Grill | Prep: 10 mins + 4 hours marinating|
Preheat: 8 mins | Cook: 8 to 12 mins | Makes: 4

INGREDIENTS:

4 lamb chops

Kosher salt to taste

1 cup plain yogurt, whole-milk

1 tsp coriander powder

1 tsp paprika

1 tsp cumin powder

½ tsp nutmeg powder

½ tsp cinnamon powder

½ tsp cardamom powder

1 tsp black pepper

1 tsp onion powder

DIRECTIONS:

1. Season the lamb chops with salt and place in a large sealable bag. In a medium bowl, mix the yogurt, coriander powder, paprika, cumin powder, nutmeg powder, cinnamon powder, cardamom powder, black pepper, and onion powder. Pour the marinade on the lamb, close the bag, and massage the marinade well onto the meat. Place the bag in the fridge and marinate for 4 hours.

2. Insert the grill grate into the Indoor Grill and close the lid. Select Grill, set the temperature to High, and the time to 12 minutes. Press Start/Stop to initiate preheating.

3. Once the Indoor Grill has preheated, open the lid and transfer the lamb chops from the marinade onto the grates while shaking off as much marinade as possible. Close the lid and cook for 8 minutes, flipping halfway. Use a meat thermometer to check for your preferred doneness; if needed cook further and check at 2-minute intervals until it is how you like it.

4. When the lamb chops are ready, transfer to a plate to rest for 3 minutes.

5. Serve afterward.

☆☆☆☆☆
Rating

Notes:

----

38. Parsley and Lemon-Grilled Veal Chops

Level: Simple / Beginner | Function: Grill | Prep: 10 mins + 4 hours marinating|
Preheat: 8 mins | Cook: 8 to 12 mins | Makes: 4

INGREDIENTS:

½ cup high smoke point oil

1 lemon, juiced

3 garlic cloves, minced

1/3 cup chopped fresh parsley

1 tbsp chopped fresh rosemary

4 veal chops, 1-inch thick

Kosher salt to taste

For garnishing:

2 garlic cloves, minced

3 tbsp chopped fresh parsley

1 tbsp fresh lemon zest

1 tsp chopped fresh rosemary

DIRECTIONS:

1. In a small bowl, mix the oil, lemon juice, garlic, parsley, and rosemary. Pat dry the chops with paper towels and season well with salt. After, rub the seasoning mix all over while pressing to adhere. Wrap the chops in plastic or place in a large freezer bag and marinate in the fridge for 6 hours.

2. Insert the grill grate into the Indoor Grill and close the lid. Select Grill, set the temperature to High, and the time to 12 minutes. Press Start/Stop to initiate preheating.

3. Once the Indoor Grill has preheated, open the lid and arrange the veal chops on the grates. Close the lid and cook for 8 minutes, flipping halfway. Use a meat thermometer to check for your preferred doneness; otherwise, cook further and check at 2-minute intervals until your desired doneness is achieved.

4. When the lamb chops are ready, transfer to a plate to rest for 3 minutes.

5. Meanwhile, in a medium bowl, mix the garnishing ingredients; garlic, parsley, lemon zest, and rosemary.

6. Sprinkle the mixture on the chops and serve afterward.

☆☆☆☆☆
Rating

Notes:

Fish & Seafood

The deep, blue has given us a bounty of fresh and exotic tastes to add to our palette! Seafood, on top of being mouth-wateringly good, is also a delicious way to add more heart-healthy meals to your day. From zesty to spicy, and perfectly served atop a bed of umami rice or grilled and seasoned vegetables for a crisp take, the flavor combinations are endless.

39. Herby Zesty Salmon

Level: Simple / Beginner | Function: Grill | Prep: 5 mins + 20 mins marinating|
Preheat: 8 mins | Cook: 7 mins (fresh)_ 12 mins (frozen) | Makes:

INGREDIENTS:

4 (5 oz) salmon fillets
2 tbsp Italian dried herbs
1 lemon, zested
½ cup dry white wine
¼ cup high smoke point oil

DIRECTIONS:

1. Place the salmon pieces in a large freezer bag. In a medium bowl, mix the herbs, lemon zest, white wine, and oil. Pour the mixture onto the salmon, close the bag, and massage the seasoning well onto the salmon.

For fresh:

2. Place the bag in the fridge and marinate for 20 minutes. Remove afterward and allow sitting to room temperature while you prepare the Indoor Grill.

3. Insert the grill grate into the Indoor Grill and close the lid. Select Grill, set the temperature to Max, and the time to 7 minutes. Press Start/Stop to initiate preheating.

4. Once the Indoor Grill has preheated, open the lid and lay the salmon pieces on the grates. Close the lid and cook for 7 minutes, flipping not necessary.

For frozen:

5. Place the bag in the freezer and marinate for 2 hours.

6. After, insert the grill grate into the Indoor Grill and close the lid. Select Grill, set the temperature to Max, and the time to 12 minutes. Press Start/Stop to initiate preheating.

7. Once the Indoor Grill has preheated, open the lid and lay the salmon pieces on the grates. Close the lid and cook for 12 minutes, flipping once or twice.

8. Once ready, transfer the cooked salmon to serving plates and enjoy immediately with summer grilled vegetables (see recipe 59).

☆☆☆☆☆
Rating

Notes:
_____
_____
_____
_____
_____

40. Cilantro-Lime Tuna Steaks

Level: Simple / Beginner | Function: Grill | Prep: 5 mins | Preheat: 8 mins |
Cook: 7 mins | Makes: 4

INGREDIENTS:

2 tbsp high smoke point oil

2 tbsp chopped fresh cilantro

1 lime, juiced

½ tsp kosher salt

¼ tsp black pepper

1 garlic clove, minced

4 (5 oz) tuna steaks

DIRECTIONS:

1. Insert the grill grate into the Indoor Grill and close the lid. Select Grill, set the temperature to Max, and the time to 7 minutes. Press Start/Stop to initiate preheating.

2. While preheating, in a medium bowl, mix the oil, cilantro, lime juice, salt, black pepper, and garlic. Brush the mixture on all sides of the tuna. (Do not marinate to prevent the lime juice from cooking the fish).

3. Once the Indoor Grill has preheated, open the lid and arrange the tuna steaks on the grate in a single layer. Close the lid and cook for 7 minutes, flipping not necessary.

4. Remove the cooked tuna onto serving plates and enjoy immediately with avocado salad.

☆☆☆☆☆
Rating

Notes:

----

41. Zesty Chili Swordfish Nuggets

Level: Simple / Beginner | Function: Air Crisp | Prep: 15 mins | Preheat: 3 mins | Cook: 12 mins | Makes: 4

INGREDIENTS:

1 ½ lb swordfish

2 cups panko breadcrumbs

½ tsp kosher salt

¼ tsp black pepper

1 small lemon, zested

½ long red chili, minced

2 eggs

High smoke point oil for spraying

DIRECTIONS:

1. Insert the crisper basket into the Indoor Grill and close the lid. Select Air Crisp, set the temperature to 390°F, the timer to 12 minutes, and press Start/Stop to initiate preheating.

2. Cut the swordfish into 1 ½-inch cubes and set aside.

3. In a shallow plate, mix the breadcrumbs, salt, black pepper, lemon zest, and red chili. Crack the eggs into a small bowl and whisk well. Coat the swordfish pieces in the egg and then generously in the breadcrumbs mixture.

4. When the Indoor Grill has preheated, open the lid, add the coated fish to the crisper basket, and spray lightly with some oil. Close the lid and cook for 12 minutes, shaking the basket twice or thrice until the nuggets are crispy and golden brown all around.

5. Transfer the fish nuggets to serving plates and enjoy warm with French fries (see side dish category).

☆☆☆☆☆
Rating

Notes:

----

42. Crunchy Tilapia Tacos

Level: Simple / Beginner | Function: Air Crisp | Prep: 15 mins | Preheat: 3 mins | Cook: 12 mins | Makes: 4

INGREDIENTS:

For the tilapia:

4 tilapia fillets

½ cup panko breadcrumbs

1 tsp fresh lemon zest

½ tsp cumin powder

1 tsp chili powder

1 tsp garlic powder

1/3 tsp kosher salt

¼ tsp black pepper

2 eggs

High smoke point oil for spraying

For assembling the tacos:

8 soft corn tortillas

2 radishes, thinly sliced

1 medium, ripe, firm avocado, pitted, peeled and cubed

1 lime, cut into wedges

Fresh cilantro leaves for topping

Hot sauce for drizzling

DIRECTIONS:

1. Insert the crisper basket into the Indoor Grill and close the lid. Select Air Crisp, set the temperature to 390°F, the timer to 12 minutes, and press Start/Stop to initiate preheating.

2. Cut the tilapia pieces into 1-inch cubes and set aside.

3. In a shallow plate, mix the breadcrumbs, lemon zest, cumin powder, chili powder, garlic powder, salt, and black pepper. In another shallow plate, crack and whisk the eggs. Coat the tilapia cubes in the egg and then generously in the breadcrumbs mixture.

4. When the Indoor Grill has preheated, open the lid, add the coated fish to the crisper basket, and spray lightly with some oil. Close the lid and cook for 12 minutes, shaking the basket twice or thrice until the fish pieces are golden brown all around.

5. Transfer the tilapia to a plate when ready and prepare the tacos.

6. Lay the tortillas on a clean, flat surface and divide the fish on top. Add the radishes, avocado, lime wedges, cilantro, and top with some hot sauce. Serve immediately.

☆☆☆☆☆
Rating

Notes:

----

43. Honey Sriracha Grilled Shrimp

Level: Simple / Beginner | Function: Grill | Prep: 15 mins + 30 mins marinating |
Preheat: 8 mins | Cook: 4 to 6 mins | Makes: 4

INGREDIENTS:

1 lb pre-frozen jumbo shrimp

2 tbsp hot smoke point oil

1 tsp chopped fresh parsley

1 tsp honey

3 tbsp Sriracha sauce

1 tbsp fresh lemon zest

½ tbsp chopped fresh cilantro for garnish

DIRECTIONS:

1. Pour the shrimp into a large bowl. In a small bowl, mix the oil, parsley, honey, Sriracha sauce, and lemon zest. Mix the marinade with the shrimp and marinate for 30 minutes. Afterward, thread the shrimp onto 2 to 3 skewers.

2. After, insert the grill grate into the Indoor Grill and close the lid. Select Grill, set the temperature to Max, and the time to 4 minutes. Press Start/Stop to initiate preheating.

3. Once the Indoor Grill preheats, open the lid and transfer the shrimp skewers onto the grates. Close the lid and cook the shrimp until the time is up, flipping not necessary. Cook an additional 1 to 2 minutes if needed.

4. Remove the shrimp onto serving plates, garnish with the cilantro and serve immediately.

☆☆☆☆☆
Rating

Notes:

----

44. Grilled Lobsters with Chili-Miso Butter

Level: Simple / Beginner | Function: Grill | Prep: 15 mins | Preheat: 3 mins |
Cook: 4 mins | Makes: 2

INGREDIENTS:

For the lobsters:

2 fresh medium lobsters

1 tsp high smoke point oil

Kosher salt and black pepper

For the chili-miso butter:

1 stick unsalted butter, melted

1 tbsp hot sauce

2 tbsp white miso

2 tbsp freshly squeezed lemon juice

1 tbsp high smoke point oil

1 tbsp finely chopped fresh chives

DIRECTIONS:

For the lobsters:

1. Insert the grill grate into the Indoor Grill and close the lid. Select Grill, set the temperature to Max, and the time to 4 minutes. Press Start/Stop to initiate preheating.
2. Meanwhile, using a lobster scissors, split the lobsters in half lengthwise through the head and tail. Scoop out and discard the yellowish-green tomalley. Also, break off and crack the claws. Drizzle the oil on the lobster pieces and season lightly with salt and black pepper.
3. Once the Indoor Grill preheats, open the lid and arrange the lobster pieces on the grates with flesh side down and the claws on the hottest part of the grate. Close the lid and cook for 4 minutes, flipping not necessary.

For the chili-miso butter:

4. Meanwhile as the lobster cooks, in a medium bowl, mix the butter, hot sauce, miso, lemon juice, oil, and chives.
5. When the lobsters are cooked, remove them onto a serving platter with the flesh side up and drizzle the butter sauce on top.
6. Enjoy the lobsters immediately.

☆☆☆☆☆
Rating

Notes:

Burgers & Sausages

Childhood wouldn't have been complete without the all-American Sunday cookout featuring juicy, char-grilled cheeseburgers loaded up with the works, and hotdogs in a warm bun just waiting to be dressed up. Now you can bring those classic flavors indoors whether it's a summer sun or a winter moon!

45. Beef and Mushroom Burger

Level: Simple / Beginner | Function: Grill | Prep: 5 mins | Preheat: 8 mins | Cook: 9 mins (fresh)_ 15 mins (frozen) | Makes: 4

INGREDIENTS:

1 lb ground beef

1/2 tsp hamburger seasoning

Kosher salt and black pepper to taste

1 tsp Worcestershire sauce

2 tbsp dry ranch dressing seasoning

High smoke point oil for brushing

4 slices cheddar cheese

4 burger rolls, split

8 bacon slices, cooked (see recipe 101)

1 large tomato, sliced into 4 rings

4 onion rings

4 small lettuce leaves

DIRECTIONS:

1. In a medium bowl, mix the beef, hamburger seasoning, salt, black pepper, Worcestershire sauce, and ranch seasoning. Mold 4 burger patties out of the mixture. For a frozen option, place the burgers in a freezer bag and freeze for at least 4 hours before cooking or use your favorite brand of pre frozen patties and brush the seasoning mixture on before placing on the grill.

2. For fresh burgers: Insert the grill grate into the Indoor Grill and close the lid. Select Grill, set the temperature to High, and the time to 9 minutes. Press Start/Stop to initiate preheating.

3. For frozen burgers: Insert the grill grate into the Indoor Grill and close the lid. Select Grill, set the temperature to Medium, and the time to 15 minutes. Press Start/Stop to initiate preheating.

4. Once the Indoor Grill has preheated, open the lid, brush one side of the patties with oil and place the patties on the grates oiled side down, brush the tops with some oil and cook for the total time, flipping 1 to 3 times during cooking.

5. A minute before the cooking time is up, open the lid and lay a cheese slice on each burger patty. Cook until the cheese melts.

6. When the burger is ready, transfer to a plate to rest for 3 minutes. Meanwhile, place the buns (with inner side down) on the grates and toast for 1 to 2 minutes.

7. Once ready, sit each burger on the bottom part of each burger bun. For each, top with 2 bacon slices, a tomato ring, an onion ring, and a lettuce leaf. Cover with the top parts of the rolls and serve immediately.

☆☆☆☆☆
Rating

Notes:

----

46. Mediterranean Beef and Pork Burger

Level: Simple / Beginner | Function: Grill | Prep: 5 mins | Preheat: 8 mins |
Cook: 9 mins (fresh)_ 15 mins (frozen) | Makes: 4

NOTE: Because these burgers include ground pork it is recommended to cook them to 160 degree internal temperature or well-done.

INGREDIENTS:

½ lb ground beef

½ lb ground pork

2 garlic cloves, minced

1 small yellow onion, finely chopped

2 tsp cumin powder

¼ tsp harissa powder

1 tsp kosher salt or to taste

½ tsp black pepper

1 large egg

2 tbsp finely chopped fresh cilantro

High smoke point oil for topping

4 burger buns, split

¼ cup crumbled feta cheese

1 medium cucumber, sliced into 16 pieces

4 lettuce leaves

Mayonnaise for topping

DIRECTIONS:

1. In a medium bowl, mix the beef, pork, garlic, onion, cumin powder, harissa powder, salt, black pepper, egg, and cilantro until well combined. Mold 4 burger patties out of the mixture. For a frozen option, place the burgers in a plastic bag and freeze until you want to have the burgers.

2. **For fresh burgers:** Insert the grill grate into the Indoor Grill and close the lid. Select Grill, set the temperature to High, and the time to 9 minutes. Press Start/Stop to initiate preheating.

3. **For frozen burgers:** Insert the grill grate into the Indoor Grill and close the lid. Select Grill, set the temperature to Medium, and the time to 15 minutes. Press Start/Stop to initiate preheating.

4. Once the Indoor Grill has preheated, open the lid, arrange the patties on top after brushing with oil, and cook for the total time, flipping 1 to 3 times during the cooking.

5. When the burger is ready, transfer to a plate to rest for 3 minutes. Meanwhile, place the bread rolls (with inner side down) on the grates and toast for 1 to 2 minutes.

6. Once the burgers are ready, place each patty on each bottom part of the burger buns. Top with the feta cheese, 2 cucumber slices each, and a lettuce leaf each. Finish with some mayonnaise and cover with the top parts of the bread.

7. Serve immediately.

☆☆☆☆☆
Rating

Notes:

----

47. Zucchini Turkey Burger

Level: Simple / Beginner | Function: Grill | Prep: 5 mins | Preheat: 8 mins |
Cook: 10 mins (fresh)_ 13 mins (frozen) | Makes: 4

INGREDIENTS:

1 lb ground turkey

1 small zucchini, finely grated and squeezed

1 garlic clove, minced

¼ cup panko breadcrumbs

1 tsp kosher salt

½ tsp black pepper

High smoke point oil for topping

4 burger buns, split

4 lettuce leaves

Mustard for topping

Ketchup for topping

DIRECTIONS:

1. In a medium bowl, mix the turkey, zucchini, garlic, breadcrumbs, salt, and black pepper. Mold 4 burger patties out of the mixture. For a frozen option, place the burgers in a plastic bag and freeze until you want to make them.

2. For fresh burgers: Insert the grill grate into the Indoor Grill and close the lid. Select Grill, set the temperature to High, and the time to 10 minutes. Press Start/Stop to initiate preheating.

3. For frozen burgers: Insert the grill grate into the Indoor Grill and close the lid. Select Grill, set the temperature to Medium, and the time to 13 minutes. Press Start/Stop to initiate preheating.

4. Once the Indoor Grill has preheated, open the lid, arrange the patties on top after brushing both sides with some oil and cook for the total time, flipping 1 to 3 times during the cook until done.

5. When the burger is ready, transfer to a plate to rest for 3 minutes. Meanwhile, place the buns (with inner side down) on the grates and toast for 1 to 2 minutes.

6. When the bread rolls are ready, lay a lettuce leaf on the bottom part of each. Top with a burger patty each when ready and then swirl some mustard and ketchup on the meat. Cover the burgers with the top bun parts and serve immediately.

☆☆☆☆☆
Rating

Notes:

----

48. Italian Sausage with Avocado Salsa

Level: Simple / Beginner | Function: Grill | Prep: 5 mins | Preheat: 8 mins |
Cook: 10 mins (fresh)_ 14 mins (frozen) | Makes: 4

INGREDIENTS:

4 large Italian sausages (fresh or frozen)

1 large avocado, pitted, peeled and chopped

1 (7 oz) can sweet corn kernels, drained

2 tomatoes, finely chopped

½ lime, juiced

¼ tsp kosher salt

¼ tsp black pepper

1 tbsp chopped fresh cilantro

2 tbsp olive oil

DIRECTIONS:

1. For fresh sausages: Insert the grill grate into the Indoor Grill and close the lid. Select Grill, set the temperature to Low, and the time to 10 minutes. Press Start/Stop to initiate preheating.

2. For frozen sausages: Insert the grill grate into the Indoor Grill and close the lid. Select Grill, set the temperature to Low, and the time to 14 minutes. Press Start/Stop to initiate preheating.

3. Once the Indoor Grill has preheated, open the lid, and arrange the sausages on the grates. Close the lid and cook until the end of the cooking time, turning 1 to 3 times.

4. As the sausages cook, in a medium bowl, mix the avocado, corn kernels, tomatoes, lime juice, salt, black pepper, cilantro, and olive oil.

5. When the sausages are ready, transfer them to serving plates and serve warm with the salsa.

☆☆☆☆☆
Rating

Notes:

---

49. BBQ Bacon & Cheddar Wrapped Hot Dogs

Level: Simple / Beginner | Function: Grill | Prep: 5 mins | Preheat: 8 mins |
Cook: 9 mins (fresh)_ 14 mins (frozen) | Makes: 4

INGREDIENTS:

4 slices cheddar cheese

4 hot dogs (fresh or frozen)

8 bacon slices

Toothpicks

½ cup BBQ sauce

4 hot dog buns

DIRECTIONS:

1. Divide the cheese slices into halves lengthwise to make 8 pieces. Wrap each hot dog from top to bottom using 2 cheese slices each and then with 2 bacon slices each. Use toothpicks to secure the ends of the bacon and cheese.

2. For fresh hot dogs: Insert the grill grate into the Indoor Grill and close the lid. Select Grill, set the temperature to Low, and the time to 9 minutes. Press Start/Stop to initiate preheating.

3. For frozen hot dogs: Insert the grill grate into the Indoor Grill and close the lid. Select Grill, set the temperature to Low, and the time to 14 minutes. Press Start/Stop to initiate preheating.

4. Once the Indoor Grill has preheated, open the lid, and arrange the hot dogs on the grates. Close the lid and cook until the end of the cook time, turning 1 to 3 times while brushing with the BBQ sauce at every check.

5. Once cooked, transfer each hot dog into each bun and serve immediately.

☆☆☆☆☆
Rating

Notes:

----

50. Hot Dogs with Kimchi Slaw and Chili Mayonnaise

Level: Simple / Beginner | Function: Grill | Prep: 5 mins | Preheat: 8 mins |
Cook: 9 mins (fresh)_ 14 mins (frozen) | Makes: 4

INGREDIENTS:

For the kimchi slaw:

1 cup kimchi, minced

1 cup grated daikon radish

2/3 cup grated carrot

4 green onions, finely chopped

½ tsp salt

For the hot dogs:

4 hot dogs

4 hot dog buns

For the chili mayonnaise:

½ cup mayonnaise

½ lime, juiced

3 tbsp chili paste

DIRECTIONS:

1. First, prepare the kimchi slaw: In a medium bowl, mix the kimchi, daikon radish, carrot, green onions, and salt. Set aside for the flavors to combine while you cook the hot dogs.

2. For fresh hot dogs: Insert the grill grate into the Indoor Grill and close the lid. Select Grill, set the temperature to Low, and the time to 9 minutes. Press Start/Stop to initiate preheating.

3. For frozen hot dogs: Insert the grill grate into the Indoor Grill and close the lid. Select Grill, set the temperature to Low, and the time to 14 minutes. Press Start/Stop to initiate preheating.

4. Once the Indoor Grill has preheated, open the lid, and arrange the hot dogs on the grates. Close the lid and cook the full time, turning 1 to 3 times.

5. While cooking, in a small bowl, mix the mayonnaise, lime juice, and chili paste until well combined.

6. When the hot dogs are ready, transfer each into the center of each bun and top with the kimchi slaw. Swirl the chili mayonnaise on top and serve immediately.

☆☆☆☆☆
Rating

Notes:

Pizza

With the following pizza recipes, pizza night can be every night if you only believe in yourself! Not to mention, you'll be joining the ranks of professional pizza dough makers in no time. Picking up a ready-made crust at the store is efficient and practical, but for the perfect dough every time, check out our steps for making your own dough from scratch. We've put together our favorite topping combinations that will make your mouth water every time. And if you're feeling extra bold, mix and match your favorite toppings for endless combinations!

Making the Pizza Crust:

Level: Simple / Beginner | Function: Grill | Prep: 15 mins + 1 hour rising | Makes: 4

INGREDIENTS:

2 ¼ tsp active dry yeast

1 ¼ cups warm water

4 cups plain flour + more for dusting

2 tsp kosher salt

¼ cup high smoke point oil + more for brushing

DIRECTIONS:

1. In a small bowl, mix the yeast and warm water; allow sitting for 15 minutes to dissolve.

2. In a large bowl, mix the flour and salt. While stirring, slowly and alternately add the yeast liquid and oil until dough forms.

3. Dust a flat surface with some flour and empty the dough on top. Knead for 2 minutes with your hands until smoothly mixed. Move the dough to a lightly oiled bowl, twice the size of the dough, and allow the dough to rise to twice its size for about 1 hour.

4. After, transfer the dough to a floured flat surface and use your hands to flatten it into an 8-inch round circle.

5. Use the dough for the following recipes.

☆☆☆☆☆
Rating

Notes:

----

51. Hot Salami Pizza

Level: Simple / Beginner | Function: Grill | Prep: 5 mins| Preheat: 8 mins |
Cook: 6 mins | Makes: 4

INGREDIENTS:

1 pizza dough

High smoke point oil for brushing

2 cups tomato sauce

1 ½ cups shredded mozzarella cheese

1 ½ cups shredded Parmesan cheese

1 ½ cups grated fontina cheese

6 oz peppered salami, thinly sliced

¾ cup roasted red bell pepper, thinly sliced

½ tsp red chili flakes

DIRECTIONS:

1. Fix the grill grate into the Indoor Grill and close the lid. Select Grill, set the temperature to Max, and the time to 6 minutes. Press Start/Stop to initiate preheating.

2. While the Indoor Grill preheats, brush the top of the dough with oil and tomato sauce. In a medium bowl, mix ½ cup of the mozzarella cheese, Parmesan cheese, and fontina cheese. Spread the cheese mix on the crust.

3. Top with the salami in a single layer, red bell pepper, chili flakes, and the remaining 1 cup mozzarella cheese.

4. Once the Indoor Grill preheats, carefully move the pizza onto the grate. Close the lid and cook for 6 minutes or until the cheeses melt.

5. Move the pizza to a clean, flat surface when ready, slice and serve afterward.

☆☆☆☆☆
Rating

Notes:

----

52. Bell Pepper and Zucchini Pizza

Level: Simple / Beginner | Function: Grill | Prep: 5 mins| Preheat: 8 mins |
Cook: 12 mins | Makes: 4

INGREDIENTS:

1 medium zucchini, thinly sliced

1 large red bell pepper, deseeded and quartered

1 large green bell pepper, deseeded and quartered

½ medium onion, thinly sliced

1 tbsp high smoke point oil + more for brushing

Kosher salt and black pepper to taste

1 pizza dough

¼ cup pizza sauce

½ cup grated mozzarella cheese

DIRECTIONS:

1. Fix the grill grate into the Indoor Grill and close the lid. Select Grill, set the temperature to Max, and the time to 10 minutes. Press Start/Stop to initiate preheating.

2. In a medium bowl, add the zucchini, bell peppers, onion, oil, salt, black pepper, and toss well.

3. Once the Indoor Grill preheats, arrange the vegetables on the grate, close the lid and cook for 10 minutes, without flipping. Transfer the ready vegetables to a plate and set aside.

4. Brush the top of the pizza dough with oil and spread the pizza sauce on top. Distribute the grilled vegetables on top and then, the mozzarella cheese.

5. Reset the Indoor Grill's time to 2 minutes, open the lid and place the pizza on top. Close the lid and cook for 2 minutes or until the cheese melts.

6. Remove the pizza afterward, allow sitting for 1 minute, then slice and serve warm.

☆☆☆☆☆
Rating

Notes:

----

53. Herbed Beef Pizza

Level: Simple / Beginner | Function: Grill | Prep: 5 mins| Preheat: 8 mins | Cook: 5 mins | Makes: 4

INGREDIENTS:

1 pizza dough

High smoke point oil for brushing

1 cup pizza sauce

2 cups shredded beef, pre-cooked (see recipe 24)

½ cup grated mozzarella cheese

Fresh basil leaves for topping

1 tbsp chopped fresh oregano for topping

DIRECTIONS:

1. Fix the grill grate into the Indoor Grill and close the lid. Select Grill, set the temperature to Max, and the time to 5 minutes. Press Start/Stop to initiate preheating.

2. Brush the top of the pizza crust with oil and spread the pizza sauce on top. Distribute the beef on the sauce, and then, the mozzarella cheese.

3. Once the Indoor Grill preheats, open the lid and place the pizza on top. Close the lid and cook for 5 minutes or until the cheese melts.

4. Remove the pizza afterward, garnish with the basil and oregano.

5. Allow sitting for 3 minutes, then slice and serve immediately

Rating

Notes:

----

54. Blue Cheese and Steak Pizza

Level: Simple / Beginner | Function: Grill | Prep: 5 mins| Preheat: 8 mins | Cook: 5 mins | Makes: 4

INGREDIENTS:

1 pizza dough

High smoke point oil for brushing

1 cup pizza sauce

2 cups shredded beef, pre-cooked (see beef recipe 24)

8 oz crumbled blue cheese

½ cup grated mozzarella cheese

Kosher salt and black pepper to taste

DIRECTIONS:

1. Fix the grill grate into the Indoor Grill and close the lid. Select Grill, set the temperature to Max, and the time to 5 minutes. Press Start/Stop to initiate preheating.

2. Brush the top of the pizza crust with oil and spread the pizza sauce on top. Distribute the beef on the sauce, then the blue cheese, mozzarella cheese, and season with some salt and black pepper.

3. Once the Indoor Grill preheats, open the lid and place the pizza on top. Close the lid and cook for 5 minutes or until the cheese melts.

4. Transfer the pizza to a chopping board afterward, allow cooling for 2 minutes, then slice and serve.

☆☆☆☆☆
Rating

Notes:

----

55. Four Cheese Pizza

Level: Simple / Beginner | Function: Grill | Prep: 5 mins| Preheat: 8 mins |
Cook: 5 mins | Makes: 4

INGREDIENTS:

2 tbsp high smoke point oil

3 garlic cloves, minced

1 pizza dough

¼ cup crumbled blue cheese

1/3 cup ricotta cheese

1 ¼ oz taleggio cheese, thinly sliced

¼ cup grated Parmesan cheese

2 tbsp chopped fresh chives

DIRECTIONS:

1. Place the grill grate in the Indoor Grill and close the lid. Select Grill, set the temperature to Max, and the time to 5 minutes. Press Start/Stop to initiate preheating.

2. In a small bowl, mix the oil and garlic. Spread the mixture on top of the pizza crust.

3. Combine the blue and ricotta cheeses in a medium bowl and spread on top of the garlic oil. Lay the taleggio cheese all over the crust and sprinkle with the Parmesan cheese.

4. Once the Indoor Grill preheats, open the lid and place the pizza on top. Close the lid and cook for 5 minutes or until the cheese melts.

5. Remove the pizza onto a flat surface when ready and garnish with the chives.

6. Slice and serve the pizza afterward.

Rating

Notes:

----

56. Herbed Ricotta White Pizza

Level: Simple / Beginner | Function: Grill | Prep: 5 mins| Preheat: 8 mins |
Cook: 5 mins | Makes: 4

INGREDIENTS:

2 tbsp high smoke point oil

3 garlic cloves, minced

1 ½ cups ricotta cheese

Kosher salt and black pepper to taste

1 tbsp chopped fresh oregano

1 tsp chopped fresh thyme

1 pizza dough

2 cups grated mozzarella cheese

¼ cup Parmigiano-Reggiano cheese

¼ tsp red chili flakes to garnish

DIRECTIONS:

1. Place the grill grate in the Indoor Grill and close the lid. Select Grill, set the temperature to Max, and the time to 5 minutes. Press Start/Stop to initiate preheating.

2. In a medium bowl, mix the oil, garlic, ricotta cheese, salt, black pepper, oregano, and thyme. Spread the mixture on the pizza crust and then, top with the remaining cheese.

3. Once the Indoor Grill preheats, open the lid and place the pizza on top. Close the lid and cook for 5 minutes or until the cheese melts.

4. When ready, transfer the pizza to a flat surface, garnish with the chili flakes, and slice.

5. Serve immediately.

Rating

Notes:

----

57. Spicy Shrimp and Bacon Pizza

Level: Simple / Beginner | Function: Grill | Prep: 5 mins| Preheat: 8 mins |
Cook: 7 mins | Makes: 4

INGREDIENTS:

1 pizza dough

¼ cup high smoke point oil

2/3 lb medium shrimp, peeled and deveined

Kosher salt and black pepper to taste

1 medium red onion, thinly sliced

2 garlic cloves, minced

8 bacon slices, cooked and crumbled

1 ½ cups grated mozzarella cheese

2 tbsp chopped fresh chives for garnish

DIRECTIONS:

1. Place the grill grate in the Indoor Grill and close the lid. Select Grill, set the temperature to Max, and the time to 7 minutes. Press Start/Stop to initiate preheating.

2. Brush the top of the pizza with oil and set aside.

3. In a medium bowl, mix the shrimp, salt, black pepper, onion, and garlic. Distribute the mixture on the pizza crust and scatter the bacon on top. Also, spread the mozzarella cheese on everything and head to the grill.

4. Once the Indoor Grill preheats, open the lid and place the pizza on top. Close the lid and cook for 7 minutes or until the cheese melts.

5. When ready, transfer the pizza to a flat surface, garnish with the chives, and slice.

6. Serve immediately.

☆☆☆☆☆
Rating

Notes:

----

58. Chicken and Black Olive Pizza

Level: Simple / Beginner | Function: Grill | Prep: 5 mins| Preheat: 8 mins |
Cook: 5 mins | Makes: 4

INGREDIENTS:

1 pizza dough

¼ cup high smoke point oil

¼ cup basil pesto

1 cup shredded leftover chicken (recipes 13 or 15 are the best bet)

1 large tomato, chopped

1 (7 oz) can sweet corn kernels, drained

½ cup sliced black olives

Kosher salt and black pepper to taste

1 cup grated mozzarella cheese

½ cup grated Parmesan cheese

DIRECTIONS:

1. Place the grill grate in the Indoor Grill and close the lid. Select Grill, set the temperature to Max, and the time to 5 minutes. Press Start/Stop to initiate preheating.

2. Brush the top of the pizza with oil and spread the pesto on top.

3. In a medium bowl, mix the chicken, tomato, corn, black olives, salt, black pepper, and spread the mixture on the pesto. Scatter the mozzarella and Parmesan cheese on the meat mix afterward.

4. Once the Indoor Grill preheats, open the lid and place the pizza on top. Close the lid and cook for 5 minutes or until the cheese melts.

5. When ready, transfer the pizza to a flat surface, allow sitting for 2 minutes, and then, slice.

6. Serve immediately.

☆☆☆☆☆
Rating

Notes:

Vegetables & Sides

Every main dish is incomplete without its trusty side dish to round out the meal. From in-season grilled veggies, to crisp or creamy potatoes, and yummy flat breads, we've laid out the best recipes to complement any dish.

59. Grilled Summer Vegetable Mix

Level: Simple / Beginner | Function: Grill | Prep: 5 mins | Preheat: 8 mins |
Cook: 10 mins | Makes: 4

INGREDIENTS

1 vine red cherry tomatoes, 5 to 6 pieces

2 potatoes, peeled and sliced into ½ -inch pieces

4 small zucchinis, sliced lengthwise into ½ -inch slices

1 lb asparagus

4 small red bell pepper, halved and deseeded

1 cup white button mushrooms

2 small bunches green onions

High smoke point oil for coating

Kosher salt and black pepper to taste

DIRECTIONS:

1. Place the grill grate into the Indoor Grill and close the lid. Select Grill, set the temperature to Max, and the time to 10 minutes. Press Start/Stop to initiate preheating.

2. Season the vegetables with oil, salt, and black pepper.

3. Once the Indoor Grill is ready, open the lid and arrange the vegetables on the grates. Close the lid and cook for 10 minutes, without flipping.

4. When ready, use tongs to transfer the vegetables to a serving platter and serve warm with your preferred main dish.

☆☆☆☆☆
Rating

Notes:

----

60. Truffle Parsley French Fries

Level: Simple/Beginner | Function: Air Crisp | Prep: 3 mins | Preheat: 3 mins | Cook: 20 to 25 mins | Makes: 4

INGREDIENTS:

4 cups frozen uncooked French fries

High smoke point oil for spraying

Sea salt to taste

1 tbsp truffle oil

1 tsp finely chopped fresh parsley

DIRECTIONS:

1. Insert the crisper basket into the Indoor Grill and close the lid. Select Air Crisp, set the temperature to 350°F, the timer to 25 minutes, and press Start/Stop to initiate preheating.

2. Once the Indoor Grill has preheated, open the lid and pour the fries into the crisper basket. Spray with some oil, close the lid and cook for 20 to 25 minutes depending on your desired doneness, shaking the basket 1 to 2 times.

3. When ready, remove the basket from the Indoor Grill and sprinkle with some salt, the truffle oil and parsley. Toss well until well coated.

4. Serve the French fries immediately.

☆☆☆☆☆
Rating

Notes:

----

61. Baked Creamy, Cheesy Brussels Sprouts with Bacon

Level: Simple/Beginner | Function: Bake & Air Crisp | Prep: 10 mins |
Preheat: 3 mins | Cook: 17 mins | Makes: 4

INGREDIENTS:

1 lb Brussel sprouts, trimmed and halved

2 tbsp melted butter

10 bacon slices, pre-cooked and chopped (see recipe 101)

5 garlic cloves, minced

1 ¼ cups heavy cream

Kosher salt and black pepper to taste

¼ cup grated Parmesan cheese

¼ cup grated mozzarella cheese

High smoke point oil

DIRECTIONS:

1. Insert the cooking pot into the Indoor Grill and close the lid. Select Bake, set the temperature to 350°F, the time to 12 minutes, and press Start/Stop to initiate preheating.

2. In a medium bowl, mix the Brussel sprouts, butter, bacon, garlic, heavy cream, salt, black, and cheeses until well distributed.

3. Once the Indoor Grill has preheated, open the lid and brush or spray the pot with some oil. Pour the mixture into the cooking pot. Carefully, use a spatula to level the food. Close the lid and bake for 12 minutes.

4. For a browned top, once the cooking time is over, reset the Indoor Grill to Air Crisp mode. Set the temperature to 375°F and set the time to 5 minutes. Cook while checking every minute or two for your desired brownness.

5. With oven mitts, remove the cooking pot, allow resting for 2 minutes and serve the dish with your preferred main meal.

☆☆☆☆☆
Rating

Notes:

----

62. Balsamic Mushroom Skewers

Level: Simple/Beginner | Function: Grill | Prep: 10 mins | Preheat: 3 mins |
Cook: 5 mins | Makes: 4

INGREDIENTS:

2 lb white button mushrooms, halved lengthwise

1 tbsp soy sauce

2 tbsp balsamic vinegar

4 garlic cloves, minced

2 tbsp high smoke point oil

1 tbsp chopped fresh parsley

DIRECTIONS:

1. Place the grill grate into the Indoor Grill and close the lid. Select Grill, set the temperature to Max, and the time to 5 minutes. Press Start/Stop to initiate preheating.

2. In a medium bowl, mix the mushrooms, soy sauce, balsamic vinegar, garlic, and oil until the mushrooms are well coated with the seasoning. On 3 to 4 skewers, thread the mushrooms.

3. Once the Indoor Grill preheats, open the lid and place the skewers on the grates. Close the lid and cook for 5 minutes or until the mushrooms are tender.

4. Transfer the mushroom skewers to serving plates afterward, garnish with the parsley, and enjoy warm with your preferred main dish.

☆☆☆☆☆
Rating

Notes:

----

63. Garlic Cheddar Biscuits

Level: Simple/Beginner | Function: Bake | Prep: 15 mins | Preheat: 3 mins |
Cook: 13 to 16 mins | Makes: 4

INGREDIENTS:

2 cups plain flour + extra for dusting

1 tsp kosher salt

1 tsp garlic powder

1 tbsp baking powder

¼ tsp granulated sugar

½ cup cold butter, diced

1 cup grated sharp cheddar cheese

1 cup milk, very cold

For topping:

¼ cup melted unsalted butter

1 tsp garlic powder

1 tbsp finely chopped fresh parsley

High smoke point oil

DIRECTIONS:

1. Insert the cooking pot into the Indoor Grill and close the lid. Select Bake, set the temperature to 380°F, the time to 16 minutes, and press Start/Stop to initiate preheating.

2. In a large bowl, mix the flour, salt, garlic powder, baking powder, and sugar. Break the cold butter into the flour mix and stir in the cheddar cheese. Slowly pour in the milk while mixing until combined. Now, use your hands to fold and mix well until well but not overly combined.

3. Dust a flat surface with some flour and move the dough on top. Tear out and form ¾-inch thick disks from the mixture.

4. For the topping, in a medium bowl, mix the butter, garlic powder, and parsley. Brush the tops of the dough disks with the mixture.

5. Once the Indoor Grill has preheated, open the lid, spray the pot with some oil and using tongs, carefully lift the dough pieces into the cooking pot. Close the lid and bake for 13 to 16 minutes or until the tops are golden brown to your taste.

6. Transfer the biscuits to a wire rack when ready and serve warm with your preferred main dish.

☆☆☆☆☆
Rating

Notes:

----

64. Rosemary Grilled Flatbread

Level: Simple/Beginner | Function: Grill | Prep: 15 mins | Preheat: 8 mins |
Cook: 16 mins | Makes: 4

INGREDIENTS:

3 cups plain flour

1 tsp instant yeast

1 tsp salt

¼ dried rosemary

4 garlic cloves, minced

1 ¼ cup warm water

¼ cup high smoke point oil + more for brushing

Flaky salt for garnish

DIRECTIONS:

1. In a large bowl, mix the flour, yeast, salt, rosemary, and garlic. Make a well in the center of the mix and pour in the warm water and oil. Gradually, mix the liquid into the dry ingredients until dough forms.

2. Flour a flat surface and transfer the dough on top. Knead with your hands until soft and smooth. Place the dough in a lightly oiled bowl, cover with plastic wrap and allow it to rise to double its size for about 1 hour.

3. After 1 hour, insert the grill grate into the Indoor Grill and close the lid. Select Grill, set the temperature to Max, the time to 16 minutes, and press Start/Stop to initiate preheating.

4. While the Indoor Grill preheats, divide the dough into 4 pieces and then flatten out into ½ -inch thickness.

5. Once the Indoor Grill has preheated, brush the grate with some oil and working in batches, place one dough per time on the grate, close the lid and cook for 4 minutes without flipping.

6. Once all the bread pieces are ready, garnish with some flaky salt, allow cooling for 2 minutes and enjoy afterward with your favorite main dish.

☆☆☆☆☆
Rating

Notes:

----

65. Herbed Honey Butternut Squash

Level: Simple/Beginner | Function: Grill | Prep: 10 mins | Preheat: 8 mins |
Cook: 14 to 16 mins | Makes: 4

INGREDIENTS:

1 (3 lb) butternut squash

1 tbsp high smoke point oil

2 tbsp honey

1 tsp Italian dried herbs

Black pepper to taste

DIRECTIONS:

1. Insert the grill grate into the Indoor Grill and close the lid. Select Grill, set the temperature to Max, the time to 14 minutes, and press Start/Stop to initiate preheating.

2. Peel the squash and cut into ½ -inch thick slices. Deseed the pieces and season with the oil, honey, herbs, and black pepper.

3. Once the Indoor Grill preheats, open the lid and arrange the squash rounds on top. Close the lid and cook for 12 to 14 minutes without flipping or until tender to your taste.

4. Transfer the squashes slices to a serving platter when ready and serve warm with your preferred main dish.

Rating

Notes:

----

66. Grilled Asparagus and Green Beans

Level: Simple/Beginner | Function: Grill | Prep: 5 mins | Preheat: 8 mins |
Cook: 5 to 7 mins | Makes: 4

INGREDIENTS:

½ lb asparagus, hard stalks trimmed

½ lb green beans, trimmed

1 tbsp high smoke point oil

1 tsp kosher salt

½ tsp black pepper

Lemon wedges for garnish

DIRECTIONS:

1. Insert the grill grate into the Indoor Grill and close the lid. Select Grill, set the temperature to Max, the time to 7 minutes, and press Start/Stop to initiate preheating.

2. In a medium bowl, toss the asparagus and green beans with oil, salt, and black pepper.

3. Once the Indoor Grill preheats, open the lid and arrange the vegetables on top in a single layer. Close the lid and cook for 5 to 7 minutes without flipping until tender to your desire.

4. Transfer the vegetables to a serving platter, garnish with lemon wedges and serve warm.

Rating

Notes:

----

67. Cilantro Sweet Potato Wedges

Level: Simple/Beginner | Function: Grill | Prep: 5 mins | Preheat: 8 mins |
Cook: 16 mins | Makes: 4

INGREDIENTS:

4 medium sweet potatoes, washed well and unpeeled

2 tbsp high smoke point oil

Kosher salt and black pepper to taste

1 tbsp chopped fresh cilantro

DIRECTIONS:

1. Insert the grill grate into the Indoor Grill and close the lid. Select Grill, set the temperature to Max, the time to 16 minutes, and press Start/Stop to initiate preheating.

2. Cut the sweet potatoes into 1-inch thick slices and season with the oil, salt, and black pepper.

3. Once the Indoor Grill preheats, open the lid and arrange the vegetable slices on the grate in a single layer. Close the lid and cook for 14 to 16 minutes or until tender, flipping halfway.

4. Dish the sweet potatoes when ready, garnish with the cilantro and serve warm.

☆☆☆☆☆
Rating

Notes:

----

68. Roasted Shrimp and Mixed Veggie Mix

Level: Simple/Beginner | Function: Bake | Prep: 10 mins | Preheat: 3 mins |
Cook: 15 mins | Makes: 4

INGREDIENTS:

1 lb medium shrimp, peeled and deveined

2 cups broccoli florets

½ medium red onion, cut into big chunks

1 large zucchini, cut into 1-inch cubes

1 large red bell pepper, deseeded and cut into 1-inch cubes

1 medium carrot, peeled and thinly sliced

2 tbsp high smoke point oil + more for brushing

1 tsp Italian seasoning

¼ tsp paprika

Kosher salt and black pepper to taste

DIRECTIONS:

1. Insert the cooking pot into the Indoor Grill and close the lid. Select Bake, set the temperature to 380°F, the time to 15 minutes, and press Start/Stop to initiate preheating.

2. In a large bowl, mix the shrimp, broccoli, onion, zucchini, bell pepper, carrot, oil, Italian seasoning, paprika, salt, and black pepper.

3. Once the Indoor Grill has preheated, open the lid and brush the pot with some. Working batches, add the ingredient mix to the cooking pot. Close the lid and cook for 13 to 15 minutes or until the vegetables are tender, mixing halfway.

4. Plate the veggie-shrimp mix when ready and serve warm.

☆☆☆☆☆
Rating

Notes:

----

69. Scallion and Butter Potato Jackets

Level: Simple/Beginner | Function: Grill | Prep: 5 mins | Preheat: 8 mins |
Cook: 16 mins | Makes: 4

INGREDIENTS:

4 large Russet potatoes

1 tsp high smoke point oil

Kosher salt and black pepper to season

4 tbsp butter, melted

2 tbsp chopped fresh scallions

DIRECTIONS:

1. Insert the grill grate into the Indoor Grill and close the lid. Select Grill, set the temperature to Max, the time to 16 minutes, and press Start/Stop to initiate preheating.

2. Season the potatoes with oil, salt, and black pepper. Use a fork to pierce all around the potatoes. Cut out a large piece of heavy-duty foil and wrap all four potatoes in the foil. Pierce a few parts of the foil to allow for quick cooking.

3. Once the Indoor Grill has preheated, open the lid and place the potato foil pack on the grate. Close the lid and cook for 14 to 16 minutes or until the potatoes are tender.

4. When ready, remove from the grill grate and allow them to cool a bit. Unwrap the foil and break the potatoes in half. Use a fork to loosen the pulp of the potatoes without scooping out.

5. Top with the butter, garnish with the scallions and serve warm.

Rating

Notes:

----

70. Grilled Mixed Sweet Peppers

Level: Simple/Beginner | Function: Grill | Prep: 5 mins | Preheat: 8 mins |
Cook: 12 mins | Makes: 4

INGREDIENTS:

½ lb small mixed bell peppers, halved and deseeded

2 tbsp high smoke point oil

Kosher salt and black pepper to taste

DIRECTIONS:

1. Insert the grill grate into the Indoor Grill and close the lid. Select Grill, set the temperature to Max, the time to 12 minutes, and press Start/Stop to initiate preheating.

2. Season the peppers with oil, salt, and black pepper.

3. Once the Indoor Grill has preheated, open the lid and arrange the peppers on the grates. Close the lid and cook the peppers for 10 to 12 minutes or until tender, flipping not needed.

4. Transfer the bell peppers to a serving platter when ready and serve warm.

☆☆☆☆☆
Rating

Notes:

----

71. Paprika Parmesan Baked Cauliflower

Level: Simple/Beginner | Function: Grill | Prep: 10 mins | Preheat: 8 mins |
Cook: 13 mins | Makes: 4

INGREDIENTS:

1 large head cauliflower, cut into florets

1 tbsp high smoke point oil

3 garlic cloves, minced

1 tsp paprika

Kosher salt and black pepper to taste

½ cup Parmesan cheese

1 tbsp chopped fresh parsley to garnish

DIRECTIONS:

1. Insert the grill grate into the Indoor Grill and close the lid. Select Grill, set the temperature to Max, the time to 13 minutes, and press Start/Stop to initiate preheating.

2. In a medium bowl, mix the cauliflower, oil, garlic, paprika, salt, and black pepper. Cut out a large piece of heavy-duty foil and pour the cauliflower mixture on the foil. Wrap into a packet and use a fork to pierce holes all around the foil.

3. Once the Indoor Grill has preheated, open the lid and place the foil pack on the grate. Close the lid and cook for 12 minutes or until the florets are tender.

4. Once ready, remove the pack from the grate, open and quickly sprinkle the Parmesan cheese on the cauliflower. Close the pack up and allow the heat to melt the cheese onto the florets for 3 to 5 minutes.

5. Open the pack, garnish with the parsley and serve the cauliflower warm.

☆☆☆☆☆
Rating

Notes:

----

72. Spicy Butter Corn on the Cob

Level: Simple/Beginner | Function: Grill | Prep: 5 mins | Preheat: 8 mins |
Cook: 13 mins | Makes: 4

INGREDIENTS:

3 tbsp melted butter

½ cup sweet chili sauce

1 tbsp hot sauce

2 limes, juiced

1 garlic clove, minced

Kosher salt and black pepper to taste

4 medium corn on the cob, husks removed

1 tbsp chopped fresh cilantro for garnish

DIRECTIONS:

1. Insert the grill grate into the Indoor Grill and close the lid. Select Grill, set the temperature to Max, the time to 13 minutes, and press Start/Stop to initiate preheating.

2. In a small bowl, mix the butter, sweet chili sauce, hot sauce, lime juice, garlic, salt, and black pepper.

3. Once the Indoor Grill has preheated, open the lid and arrange the corn on the grate. Close the lid and cook for 13 minutes, turning every 2 minutes and basting with the sauce.

4. Once ready, transfer the corn to a serving platter, garnish with the cilantro and serve warm.

☆☆☆☆☆
Rating

Notes:

----

73. Soy Grilled Eggplants with Sesame Seeds

Level: Simple/Beginner | Function: Grill | Prep: 5 mins | Preheat: 8 mins |
Cook: 12 mins | Makes: 4

INGREDIENTS:

¼ cup high smoke point oil

1 tbsp soy sauce

1 tbsp fresh ginger paste

1 tsp rice vinegar

1 tsp sesame oil

4 large eggplants, cut into 1-inch rounds

Toasted sesame seeds for garnish

1 tbsp chopped fresh cilantro for garnish

DIRECTIONS:

1. Insert the grill grate into the Indoor Grill and close the lid. Select Grill, set the temperature to Max, the time to 12 minutes, and press Start/Stop to initiate preheating.

2. In a small bowl, mix the oil, soy sauce, ginger paste, rice vinegar, and sesame oil.

3. Once the Indoor Grill has preheated, open the lid and arrange the eggplant pieces on the grate. Brush the top with some of the sauce, close the lid and cook for 12 minutes, flipping halfway and basting the other side.

4. Once ready, dish the eggplants, garnish with the sesame seeds, cilantro, and serve immediately.

☆☆☆☆☆
Rating

Notes:

----

74. Foil Grilled Onions

Level: Simple/Beginner | Function: Grill | Prep: 10 mins | Preheat: 8 mins |
Cook: 12 mins | Makes: 4

INGREDIENTS:

1 ½ cups pearl onions, peeled

¼ cup sun-dried tomatoes, soaked in hot water, drained and chopped

2 tbsp high smoke point oil

1 tbsp chopped fresh thyme

Kosher salt and black pepper to taste

DIRECTIONS:

1. Insert the grill grate into the Indoor Grill and close the lid. Select Grill, set the temperature to Max, the time to 12 minutes, and press Start/Stop to initiate preheating.

2. Prepare a wide cut of heavy-duty foil and set aside. In a medium bowl, mix the onions, tomatoes, oil, thyme, salt, and black pepper. Pour the mixture onto the foil and wrap to seal. No need to pierce holes on the foil.

3. Once the Indoor Grill has preheated, open the lid and place the foil packet on the grate. Close the lid and cook for 12 minutes or until the onions are tender.

4. After cooking, remove the foil pack onto a serving platter and carefully open the foil.

5. Serve the dish warm with your desired main dish.

☆☆☆☆☆
Rating

Notes:

----

75. Foil-Roasted Whole Garlic

Level: Simple/Beginner | Function: Grill | Prep: 2 mins | Preheat: 8 mins |
Cook: 12 mins | Makes: 4

INGREDIENTS:

4 large heads garlic

1 tbsp high smoke point oil

Kosher salt and black pepper to taste

DIRECTIONS:

1. Insert the grill grate into the Indoor Grill and close the lid. Select Grill, set the temperature to Max, the time to 12 minutes, and press Start/Stop to initiate preheating.

2. Prepare a medium cut of heavy-duty foil and set aside. Slice off the top head of the garlic bulbs and arrange on the foil. Drizzle the oil on top and season with salt and black pepper. Wrap the foil and pierce a few holes on the foil using a fork.

3. Once the Indoor Grill has preheated, open the lid and place the foil packet on the grate. Close the lid and cook for 12 minutes or until the garlic cloves are tender.

4. After cooking, remove the foil pack onto a serving platter and carefully open the foil.

5. Serve the dish warm with your preferred main dish.

☆☆☆☆☆
Rating

Notes:

----

76. Balsamic Tomato, Pepper, and Zucchini Mix

Level: Simple/Beginner | Function: Grill | Prep: 2 mins | Preheat: 8 mins |
Cook: 12 mins | Makes: 4

INGREDIENTS:

2 cups cherry tomatoes, halved

1 large red bell pepper, deseeded and diced

1 large yellow bell pepper, deseeded and diced

4 medium zucchinis

1 tbsp balsamic vinegar

1 ½ tbsp high smoke point oil

Kosher salt and black pepper to taste

DIRECTIONS:

1. Insert the grill grate into the Indoor Grill and close the lid. Select Grill, set the temperature to Max, the time to 12 minutes, and press Start/Stop to initiate preheating.

2. Prepare a large cut of heavy-duty foil and set aside. In a medium bowl, mix the tomatoes, bell peppers, zucchinis, balsamic vinegar, oil, salt, and black pepper. Pour the mixture on the foil and wrap up into a packet.

3. Once the Indoor Grill has preheated, open the lid and place the foil packet on the grate. Close the lid and cook for 12 minutes or until the vegetables are tender.

4. After cooking, transfer the foil to a serving platter and carefully open the foil.

5. Serve the dish warm with your preferred main dish.

☆☆☆☆☆
Rating

Notes:

Appetizers & Snacks

Preface your meal with one of these appetizers, and stave away the munchies during the day with these perfectly-sized snack options to get you through that afternoon slump.

77. Olive and Tomato Bruschetta

Level: Simple / Beginner | Function: Grill | Prep: 10 mins + 1 hour chilling | Preheat: 8 mins | Cook: 3 mins | Makes: 4 – 6

INGREDIENTS:

2 medium firm, ripe tomatoes, deseeded and chopped

2 tbsp chopped fresh basil

¼ cup sliced Kalamata olives

1 tbsp high smoke point oil + more for brushing

2 tsp balsamic vinegar

1 tbsp finely chopped red onion

Sea salt and black pepper to taste

16 slices baguette, cut at slight angle

DIRECTIONS:

1. Place the grill grate into the Indoor Grill and close the lid. Select Grill, set the temperature to Max, and the time to 3 minutes. Press Start/Stop to initiate preheating.

2. Meanwhile, in a medium bowl, combine the tomatoes, basil, olives, 1 tbsp of oil, balsamic vinegar, onion, salt, and black pepper. Cover the bowl with plastic wrap and set aside in the fridge for 1 hour. Also, brush the bread on both sides with some oil.

3. Once the Indoor Grill is ready, open the lid and arrange the bread pieces on the grate. Close the lid and cook for 3 minutes, without flipping.

4. When ready, use tongs to transfer the bread pieces to a serving platter. Take out the tomato mixture from the fridge and spoon the topping on the bread.

5. Serve immediately.

☆☆☆☆☆
Rating

Notes:

----

78. BBQ Smokies Skewers

Level: Simple / Beginner | Function: Grill | Prep: 5 mins | Preheat: 8 mins |
Cook: 5 mins | Makes: 4 – 6

INGREDIENTS:

36 cocktail sausages

½ cup BBQ sauce

3 tbsp honey

Toothpicks

DIRECTIONS:

1. Place the grill grate into the Indoor Grill and close the lid. Select Grill, set the temperature to Max, and the time to 5 minutes. Press Start/Stop to initiate preheating.

2. Meanwhile, in a medium bowl, add the smokies and toss with the BBQ sauce, and honey until well-coated. After, thread the smokies on 4 skewers (9 per piece).

3. Once the Indoor Grill is ready, open the lid and place the skewers on top. Close the lid and cook for 5 minutes, turning once.

4. Once the smokies have cooked, transfer to a serving platter and remove the skewers.

5. Insert toothpicks into the smokies and serve warm.

☆☆☆☆☆
Rating

Notes:

----

79. Bacon Wrapped Cheddar

Level: Simple / Beginner | Function: Air Crisp | Prep: 10 mins | Preheat: 3 mins | Cook: 10 mins | Makes: 4 – 6

INGREDIENTS:

16 cubes cheddar cheese

16 bacon slices

Toothpicks

DIRECTIONS:

1. Insert the crisper basket into the Indoor Grill and close the lid. Select Air Crisp, set the temperature to 350°F, and the time to 10 minutes. Press Start/Stop to initiate preheating.

2. While the Indoor Grill preheats, wrap each cheese cube with each bacon slice and secure the bacon ends with a toothpick.

3. Once the Indoor Grill is ready, open the lid and add the wrapped cheeses to the crisper basket. Close the lid and cook for 10 minutes or until the bacon is brown, crispy, and the cheese melted.

4. Transfer the pieces to a serving platter when ready and enjoy warm.

☆☆☆☆☆
Rating

Notes:

----

80. Beef and Veggie Samosas

Level: Simple / Beginner | Function: Bake & Air Crisp | Prep: 10 mins |
Preheat: 3 mins | Cook: 35 mins | Makes: 4

INGREDIENTS:

½ lb ground beef

1 potato, peeled and cut into tiny cubes

1 tbsp cumin powder

1 tbsp turmeric powder

½ cup onion, chopped

1 tsp fresh ginger paste

1 tsp minced garlic

2 tbsp minced serrano chili

1 cup minced carrots

1 tbsp high smoke point oil + more for spraying

Kosher salt and black pepper to taste

½ lb frozen peas

1 package large wonton wrappers

1 whole egg, beaten

DIRECTIONS:

1. Insert the cooking pot into the Indoor Grill and close the lid. Select Bake, set the temperature to 380°F, and the time to 15 minutes. Press Start/Stop to initiate preheating.

2. While the Indoor Grill preheats, in a medium bowl, mix the beef, potato, cumin powder, turmeric powder, onion, ginger paste, garlic, serrano chili, carrots, oil, salt, and black pepper.

3. Once the Indoor Grill is ready, open the lid, brush the pot with some oil, and spoon the mixture into the cooking pot. Use a spatula to level the top, close the lid and cook for 15 minutes or until the beef is brown and the vegetables soften, turning halfway.

4. When ready, with oven mitts, remove the cooking pot and mix in the peas. Spread the beef mixture on a wide plate and set aside to cool completely.

5. Once cooled, start making the samosas.

6. Insert the cooking pot with the crisper basket into the Indoor Grill and close the lid. Select Air Crisp, set the temperature to 360°F, and the time to 20 minutes. Press Start/Stop to initiate preheating.

7. Lay a wonton wrapper on a flat surface, add 2 tbsp of the beef filling to the center, and wrap into a fitted triangle. Brush the ends of the wrapper with egg and seal.

8. Once all the samosa triangles are ready and Indoor Grill preheated, open the lid and place the samosa pieces in the crisper basket. Close the lid and cook for 18 to 20 minutes, depending on your desired brownness and crispiness, flipping once.

☆☆☆☆☆
Rating

Notes:

----

81. Bacon-Wrapped Jalapeno Poppers

Level: Simple / Beginner | Function: Air Crisp | Prep: 10 mins | Preheat: 3 mins | Cook: 10 mins | Makes: 4

INGREDIENTS:

8 large jalapeno peppers

8 tbsp cream cheese, room temperature

1/3 lb grated Monterey Jack cheese

16 bacon slices

DIRECTIONS:

1. Insert the crisper basket into the Indoor Grill and close the lid. Select Air Crisp, set the temperature to 360°F, and the time to 10 minutes. Press Start/Stop to initiate preheating.

2. While the Indoor Grill preheats, cut the jalapeno peppers in half and deseed them. Mix the cream cheese and Monterey Jack cheese in a small bowl and fill the peppers halves with the mixture. Then, wrap each stuffed half pepper with two bacon slices.

3. Once the Indoor Grill has preheated, open the lid and arrange the peppers in the crisper basket. Close the lid and cook for 10 minutes.

4. Transfer the ready poppers to a plate when ready and serve warm.

☆☆☆☆☆
Rating

Notes:

---

82. Sweet Goat Cheese Balls

Level: Simple / Beginner | Function: Air Crisp | Prep: 10 mins | Preheat: 3 mins | Cook: 10 mins | Makes: 4

INGREDIENTS:

8 oz log soft goat cheese

½ cup panko breadcrumbs

1 egg, beaten

High smoke point oil for spraying

¼ cup honey for drizzling

DIRECTIONS:

1. Insert the crisper basket into the Indoor Grill and close the lid. Select Air Crisp, set the temperature to 375°F, and the time to 10 minutes. Press Start/Stop to initiate preheating.

2. Cut the goat cheese into 24 pieces and mold into balls. Roll each ball in the egg and then, generously in the breadcrumbs.

3. Once the Indoor Grill has preheated, open the lid, put the coated cheese in the crisper basket, and spray with a little oil. Close the lid and cook for 10 minutes or until golden brown and crispy.

4. Transfer the ready cheese balls to a serving platter and drizzle with the honey.

5. Serve afterward.

☆☆☆☆☆
Rating

Notes:

---

83. Asian Chili Tater Tots

Level: Simple / Beginner | Function: Air Crisp | Prep: 10 mins | Preheat: 3 mins | Cook: 20 mins | Makes: 4 – 6

INGREDIENTS:

16 oz frozen herbed tater tots

½ cup sour cream

3 toasted nori sheets, chopped

1 tsp chopped fresh parsley

4 tbsp chili sauce

2 scallions, chopped

DIRECTIONS:

1. Insert the crisper basket into the Indoor Grill and close the lid. Select Air Crisp, set the temperature to 360°F, and the time to 20 minutes. Press Start/Stop to initiate preheating.

2. Once the Indoor Grill has preheated, open the lid, and pour the tater tots into the crisper basket. Close the lid and cook between 18 to 20 minutes or until golden brown.

3. Meanwhile, in a small bowl, mix the mayonnaise, nori, parsley, chili sauce, and scallions.

4. Once the tater tots are ready, transfer the snacks to a serving platter and top with the mayonnaise sauce. Serve immediately.

☆☆☆☆☆
Rating

Notes:

----

84. Dried Mixed Fruits

Level: Simple / Beginner | Function: Dehydrate | Prep: 10 mins | Preheat: 3 mins | Cook: 8 hours | Makes: 4 – 6

INGREDIENTS:

1 large green apple, thinly sliced and deseeded

1 cup strawberry, thinly sliced

1 small pineapple, thinly sliced

1 medium ripe mango, thinly sliced

3 kiwis, peeled and thinly sliced

DIRECTIONS:

1. Insert the crisper basket into the Indoor Grill and close the lid. Select Dehydrate, set the temperature to 135°F, and the time to 8 hours. Press Start/Stop to initiate preheating.

2. Once the Indoor Grill has preheated, open the lid, and pour the fruits into the crisper basket. Close the lid and cook for 8 hours.

3. Transfer the fruits into serving bowls and enjoy!

☆☆☆☆☆
Rating

Notes:

----

85. Parmesan Coated Potato Chips

Level: Simple / Beginner | Function: Air Crisp | Prep: 10 mins | Preheat: 3 mins | Cook: 20 mins | Makes: 4 – 6

INGREDIENTS:

2 large red potatoes, peeled and thinly sliced

Kosher salt to taste

4 garlic cloves, minced

2 tbsp grated Parmesan cheese

DIRECTIONS:

1. Insert the crisper basket into the Indoor Grill and close the lid. Select Air Crisp, set the temperature to 375°F, and the time to 20 minutes. Press Start/Stop to initiate preheating.

2. Meanwhile, pat dry the potatoes and put them in a large bowl. Sprinkle with the salt, garlic, Parmesan cheese, and toss until the potatoes are well coated.

3. Once the Indoor Grill has preheated, open the lid, and working in batches, pour the potatoes into the crisper basket making sure not to overcrowd. Close the lid and cook for 18 to 20 minutes or until the potatoes are golden brown and crispy.

4. Transfer the potatoes to serving bowls and enjoy!

☆☆☆☆☆
Rating

Notes:

----

86. Strawberry Oatmeal Bars

Level: Simple / Beginner | Function: Bake | Prep: 5 mins | Preheat: 3 mins |
Cook: 25 mins | Makes: 4 – 6

INGREDIENTS:

1 cup rolled oats

¾ cup wheat flour

¼ tsp ginger powder

1/3 cup light brown sugar

6 tbsp unsalted butter

¼ tsp kosher salt

1 tsp cornstarch

2 cups strawberries, diced into small pieces

1 tbsp white sugar

1 tbsp freshly squeezed lemon juice

High smoke point oil for brushing

DIRECTIONS:

1. Insert the cooking pot into the Indoor Grill and close the lid. Select Bake, set the temperature to 375°F, and the time to 25 minutes. Press Start/Stop to initiate preheating.

2. Meanwhile, in a medium bowl, mix the oats, wheat flour, ginger, brown sugar, butter, salt, cornstarch, strawberries, white sugar, and lemon juice.

3. Once the Indoor Grill has preheated, open the lid, brush pot with some oil, and spread the oat mixture in the cooking pot. Use the spatula to level the top evenly. Close the lid and bake for 25 minutes or until firm, and compacted.

4. When the timer ends, open the lid and use oven mitts to remove the cooking pot and flip the contents onto a chopping board.

5. Cut the snack into bars, cool completely at room temperature or in the refrigerator and enjoy afterward.

☆☆☆☆☆
Rating

Notes:

----

87. Granola Chocolate Chip Squares

Level: Simple / Beginner | Function: Bake | Prep: 5 mins | Preheat: 3 mins |
Cook: 25 mins | Makes: 4 – 6

INGREDIENTS:

2 cups granola

½ cup unsweetened shredded
  coconut

¼ tsp salt

1 egg, beaten

½ cup unsalted butter

¼ cup coconut oil

1/3 cup honey

2 tsp vanilla extract

½ cup chocolate chips

DIRECTIONS:

1. Insert the cooking pot into the Indoor Grill and close the lid. Select Bake, set the temperature to 375°F, and the time to 25 minutes. Press Start/Stop to initiate preheating.

2. Meanwhile, in a medium bowl, mix the granola, coconut, salt, butter, coconut oil, honey, and vanilla extract. Fold in the chocolate chips afterward.

3. Once the Indoor Grill has preheated, open the lid and spread the granola mixture in the cooking pot. Use the spatula to level the top evenly. Close the lid and bake for 25 minutes or until firm, and compacted.

4. When the timer is up, open the lid and use oven mitts to remove the cooking pot and flip the contents onto a chopping board.

5. Cut into bars, allow complete cooling and enjoy afterward.

☆☆☆☆☆
Rating

Notes:

----

88. Garlic and Mozzarella Pretzels

Level: Simple / Beginner | Function: Bake | Prep: 5 mins | Preheat: 3 mins |
Cook: 8 mins | Makes: 4 – 6

INGREDIENTS:

1 pkg crescent refrigerator rolls

½ cup melted butter

2 tsp minced garlic

½ cup grated mozzarella cheese

High smoke point oil for brushing

DIRECTIONS:

1. Insert the cooking pot into the Indoor Grill and close the lid. Select Bake, set the temperature to 350°F, and the time to 8 minutes. Press Start/Stop to initiate preheating.

2. Unwrap the crescent roll and slice the dough lengthwise into 1-inch strips. Roll each strip into 12-inch logs of ½ -inch thinness. Shape the rolls into pretzel pieces and sit on the flat surface with twisted sides up.

3. In a small bowl, mix the butter, garlic, and brush the mix on top of the pretzel dough. Sprinkle the mozzarella cheese on top afterward.

4. Once the Indoor Grill preheats, open the lid, brush or spray the pot with some oil and using tongs, and working in batches, arrange the pretzels in the cooking pot with twisted sides up. Close the lid and bake for 8 minutes.

5. Once ready, transfer the pretzels to a serving platter, allow complete cooling and enjoy!

Rating

Notes:

----

89. Crispy Salted Cumin Chickpeas

Level: Simple / Beginner | Function: Air Crisp| Prep: 5 mins | Preheat: 3 mins | Cook: 10 mins | Makes: 4

INGREDIENTS:

1 (14 oz) can chickpeas, drained and rinsed

½ tsp cumin powder

1 tbsp high smoke point oil

Kosher salt to taste

DIRECTIONS:

1. Insert the crisper basket into the Indoor Grill and close the lid. Select Bake, set the temperature to 390°F, and the time to 10 minutes. Press Start/Stop to initiate preheating.

2. Meanwhile, pat dry the chickpeas with paper towels and pour into a medium bowl. Toss the chickpeas with the cumin powder, oil, and salt until well-coated.

3. Once the Indoor Grill has preheated, open the lid and pour the chickpeas into the crisper basket. Close the lid and cook for 10 minutes or until the chickpeas are golden brown.

4. Once ready, transfer the chickpeas to serving bowls, allow cooling and enjoy afterward.

Rating

Notes:

----

90. Spicy Texas Beef Jerky

Level: Simple/Beginner | Function: Dehydrate | Prep: 10 mins + 6 hour marinating | Preheat: 3 mins | Cook: 7 hours | Makes: 4 – 6

INGREDIENTS:

1 lb flank steak, partially frozen and cut against the grain into ¼ - inch slices

½ cup water

1 cup Worcestershire sauce

4 tsp chili powder

4 garlic cloves, minced

2 tsp chipotle powder

1 tsp cayenne pepper

1 tsp salt

2 tsp black pepper

DIRECTIONS:

1. Place the beef in a large zipper bag. In a medium bowl, mix the water, Worcestershire sauce, chili powder, garlic, chipotle powder, cayenne pepper, salt, and black pepper. Pour the marinade over the beef, close the bag and place the bag in the fridge for 6 hours to marinate.

2. After 6 hours of marinating, insert the crisper basket into the Indoor Grill and close the lid. Select Dehydrate, set the temperature to 150°F, and the time to 7 hours. Press Start/Stop to initiate preheating.

3. Remove the bag from the fridge, take out the meat onto a flat surface and pat the beef dry with paper towels.

4. Once the Indoor Grill has preheated, open the lid and pour the beef into the crisper basket. Close the lid and cook for 7 hours or until the meat is dried to your taste.

5. Remove the meat onto a serving platter, allow cooling and enjoy.

Rating

Notes:

Desserts

Who can resist the temptation of a decadent dessert to finish off the day? The Indoor Grill is more than a haven for tender steaks and flaky fish. It's also the perfect tool to satisfy that ever craving sweet tooth.

91. Air Fried Oreos

Level: Simple / Beginner | Function: Air Crisp | Prep: 5 mins | Preheat: 3 mins | Cook: 5 mins | Makes: 4

INGREDIENTS:

2 pkg crescent dough sheet

16 Oreo cookies (or experiment with other types of cookies!)

High smoke point oil for spraying

Confectioner's sugar for dusting

DIRECTIONS:

1. Place the crisper basket into the Indoor Grill and close the lid. Select Air Crisp, set the temperature to 360°F, and the time to 5 minutes. Press Start/Stop to initiate preheating.

2. Spread out the crescent dough sheets into large rectangles and using a knife, cut into 16 pieces. Wrap each Oreo with a dough piece and press the dough onto the cookie to hold.

3. Once the Indoor Grill is ready, open the lid, spray the basket with some oil, arrange the wrapped cookies in the crisper basket and spray lightly with oil. Close the lid and cook for 5 minutes or until golden brown, shaking once.

4. Once ready, remove the Oreos onto a plate and allow complete cooling.

5. Garnish with the confectioner's sugar and enjoy!

Rating

Notes:

----

92. Air Fried S'mores

Level: Simple / Beginner | Function: Air Crisp | Prep: 5 mins | Preheat: 3 mins | Cook: 5 mins | Makes: 4

INGREDIENTS:

16 egg roll wrappers, small size

½ cup marshmallow cream

1 medium chocolate bar, cut into 8 pieces

¼ cup crushed graham crackers for sprinkling

1 egg, beaten with 1 tsp of water

High smoke point oil for spraying

DIRECTIONS:

1. Place the crisper basket into the Indoor Grill and close the lid. Select Air Crisp, set the temperature to 360°F, and the time to 5 minutes. Press Start/Stop to initiate preheating.

2. Lay one egg roll wrapper on a clean, flat surface. Place a chocolate cube on top, then add 1 tbsp of marshmallow cream on the chocolate and sprinkle with some graham cracker crumbs. Cover with another egg roll wrapper and seal the edges using the egg as sealant.

3. Once the Indoor Grill is ready, open the lid, spray lightly with some oil, and arrange the dessert pieces in the crisper basket. Spray the food with a little oil, close the lid and cook for 5 minutes or until golden brown, flipping once.

4. Transfer the dessert to a serving plate when ready, allow cooling and enjoy afterward.

Rating

Notes:

----

93. New Yorker Cheesecake

Level: Simple / Beginner | Function: Bake | Prep: 15 mins + 4 hour 30 mins chilling|
Preheat: 3 mins | Cook: 50 to 60 mins | Makes: 4

INGREDIENTS:

2 cups graham crackers, crushed

1/3 cup melted butter

16 oz cream cheese, room temperature

1 cup granulated sugar

2 tsp lemon zest

½ tsp vanilla extract

2 tbsp plain flour

4 eggs

1 cup sour cream

Frozen raspberries for garnish

8-inch springform pan

DIRECTIONS:

1. Line an 8-inch springform pan with parchment paper and set aside. In a medium bowl, mix the graham crackers and butter until well combined. Spread the mixture in the springform pan, cover the pan with plastic wrap and refrigerate for 30 minutes.

2. After, without any inserted accessories, preheat the Indoor Grill. Select Bake, set the temperature to 350°F, and the time to 60 minutes. Press Start/Stop to initiate preheating.

3. In a large bowl using electric beaters, whisk the cream cheese and sugar until smooth. Add the lemon zest, vanilla, flour, and whisk until smooth. While still beating, add the eggs one after another until well mixed. Then, finally mix in the sour cream.

4. Remove the pan from the fridge, take off the plastic wrap and pour the cream mixture onto the crust using a spoon to level the top and gently tapping the top to release small air bubbles.

5. Once the Indoor Grill has preheated, open the lid and sit the pan on the base. Close the lid and bake for 60 minutes or until the cake is set in the center.

6. Once ready, turn the Indoor Grill off and leave the cake in there with the lid closed to cool completely to prevent the cheesecake from cracking.

7. Transfer the cake to the fridge afterward and chill for 4 hours.

8. After 4 hours, remove the cake from the fridge and release the cake pan. Garnish the cake with as many raspberries as you like.

9. Slice and serve immediately.

☆☆☆☆☆
Rating

Notes:

----

94. Grilled Apple Pie

Level: Simple / Beginner | Function: Grill | Prep: 10 mins | Preheat: 3 mins |
Cook: 27 mins | Makes: 4

INGREDIENTS:

6 red apples, cored and quartered

¼ cup granulated sugar

1 tbsp cornstarch

1 refrigerated pie crust

ACCESSORIES:

8-inch baking pan

DIRECTIONS:

1. Insert the grill grate into the Indoor Grill. Select Grill, set the temperature to Max, and the time to 7 minutes. Press Start/Stop to initiate preheating.

2. In a medium bowl, mix the apples, sugar, and cornstarch.

3. Once the Indoor Grill has preheated, open the lid and arrange the apples on the grate. Close the lid and cook for 7 minutes, flipping not necessary.

4. When the apples are ready, place them on a cutting board, chop them, and then, transfer to an 8-inch baking pan. Lay the pie crust directly over the filling and pinch the ends to adhere to the pan. Using a knife, cut 4 to 6 Xs in the dough to allow steam escape during baking.

5. Remove the grill grate from the Indoor Grill. Close the lid, select bake, set the temperature to 350°F, and set the time to 20 minutes. Select Start/Stop to initiate preheating.

6. Once the Indoor Grill has preheated, open the lid and place the baking pan on the base. Close the lid and cook for 20 minutes.

7. When ready, remove the baking pan and allow the pie to cool completely.

8. Serve the pie with ice cream.

☆☆☆☆☆
Rating

Notes:

_____

_____

_____

_____

_____

95. Grilled Peaches with Cinnamon Butter and Ice Cream

Level: Simple / Beginner | Function: Grill | Prep: 5 mins | Preheat: 8 mins |
Cook: 7 mins | Makes: 4

INGREDIENTS:

1 stick butter, melted

2 tbsp granulated sugar

1 tsp cinnamon powder

A pinch salt

4 ripe peaches, halved and pitted

High smoke point oil for topping

Vanilla ice cream for topping

Mint leaves to garnish

DIRECTIONS:

1. Insert the grill grate into the Indoor Grill. Select Grill, set the temperature to Max, and the time to 7 minutes. Press Start/Stop to initiate preheating.

2. In a medium bowl, mix the butter, sugar, and cinnamon powder. Set aside. Also, brush the peaches with oil.

3. Once the Indoor Grill has preheated, open the lid and arrange the peaches (inner side down) on the grate. Close the lid and cook for 7 minutes, flipping not necessary.

4. When the peaches are ready, transfer to a serving platter, pour the cinnamon butter on top, add some ice cream and garnish with the mint leaves.

5. Serve immediately.

☆☆☆☆☆
Rating

Notes:

----

96. Grilled Pineapple Sundae
with Walnuts

Level: Simple / Beginner | Function: Grill | Prep: 10 mins | Preheat: 8 mins |
Cook: 7 mins | Makes: 4

INGREDIENTS:

For the grilled pineapples:

High smoke oil point for brushing

2 small pineapples, peeled, cored, and sliced into 2-inch rings

2 tbsp brown sugar

For the fudge sauce:

1 (7 oz) can sweetened condensed milk, warmed

½ cup heavy cream, warmed

1 tbsp butter, melted

1/3 cup cocoa powder, sifted

For assembling:

Vanilla ice cream

Whipped cream

1 tbsp chopped walnuts

DIRECTIONS:

1. Insert the grill grate into the Indoor Grill. Select Grill, set the temperature to Max, and the time to 7 minutes. Press Start/Stop to initiate preheating.

2. In a medium bowl, sprinkle the pineapple slices with the brown sugar.

3. Once the Indoor Grill has preheated, open the lid, brush or spray the grates with some oil, and arrange the pineapples on the grate. Close the lid and cook for 7 minutes, flipping not necessary.

4. Meanwhile, make the fudge sauce. In a small bowl, vigorously whisk the condensed milk, heavy cream, butter, and cocoa powder until smooth. Set aside.

5. When the pineapples are ready, transfer the pieces to dessert plates and top with the vanilla ice cream, whipped cream, fudge sauce, and walnuts.

6. Serve immediately.

☆☆☆☆☆
Rating

Notes:

----

97. Grilled Doughnuts with Espresso Coconut Glaze

Level: Simple / Beginner | Function: Grill | Prep: 10 mins | Preheat: 8 mins |
Cook: 4 mins | Makes: 6

INGREDIENTS:

6 (1 day-old) large doughnuts, halved through the middle

¼ cup heavy cream

2 tbsp strongly brewed espresso

1 cup powdered sugar

2 tbsp unsweetened coconut shavings

DIRECTIONS:

1. Insert the grill grate into the Indoor Grill. Select Grill, set the temperature to Max, and the time to 4 minutes. Press Start/Stop to initiate preheating.

2. Once the Indoor Grill has preheated, open the lid and arrange the doughnuts on the grate with the inner side down. Close the lid and cook for 4 minutes, flipping not necessary.

3. Meanwhile, in a small bowl, whisk the heavy cream, espresso, sugar, and coconut shavings. Set aside.

4. When the doughnuts are ready, transfer them to a serving platter and swirl the coffee glaze on top.

5. Serve.

Rating

Notes:

----

98. Grilled Strawberry Shortcake Skewers

Level: Simple / Beginner | Function: Grill | Prep: 10 mins | Preheat: 8 mins |
Cook: 4 mins | Makes: 4

INGREDIENTS:

For the skewers:

1 pound-cake, cut into 2-inch cubes

32 small strawberries, hulled

2 tbsp high smoke point oil

2 tbsp honey

For the cream sauce:

1 cup heavy cream

1 tsp fresh lemon zest

2 tbsp granulated sugar

DIRECTIONS:

1. Insert the grill grate into the Indoor Grill. Select Grill, set the temperature to Max, and the time to 4 minutes. Press Start/Stop to initiate preheating.

2. On 4 skewers, alternately thread the cake cubes and strawberries. After, brush the skewers with the oil and honey.

3. Once the Indoor Grill has preheated, open the lid and arrange the skewers on the grate. Close the lid and cook for 4 minutes, flipping not necessary.

4. Meanwhile, in a small bowl, whisk the heavy cream, lemon zest, and sugar until well combined.

5. Transfer the skewers to a serving platter when ready to cool completely and then swirl the sauce on top.

6. Serve.

Rating

Notes:

----

99. Grilled Bananas with Caramel Drizzle

Level: Simple / Beginner | Function: Grill | Prep: 10 mins | Preheat: 8 mins |
Cook: 3 mins | Makes: 4

INGREDIENTS:

12 ripe bananas, peeled and halved lengthwise

1 cup caramel sauce

DIRECTIONS:

1. Insert the grill grate into the Indoor Grill. Select Grill, set the temperature to Max, and the time to 3 minutes. Press Start/Stop to initiate preheating.

2. Once the Indoor Grill has preheated, open the lid and arrange the bananas on the grate with the inner side down. Close the lid and cook for 3 minutes, flipping not necessary.

3. When the bananas are ready, transfer to a serving platter and drizzle the caramel sauce on top.

4. Serve.

Rating

Notes:

----

100. Pecan Brownies

Level: Simple / Beginner | Function: Bake| Prep: 10 mins | Preheat: 3 mins |
Cook: 25 mins | Makes: 4

INGREDIENTS:

½ cup butter

2 eggs

2 tsp vanilla extract

¼ cup cocoa powder

1 cup brown sugar

¼ cup plain flour

1/8 tsp sea salt

½ cup chopped pecans

8-inch springform pan

DIRECTIONS:

1. Preheat the Indoor Grill without any insert unit. Select Bake, set the temperature to 320°F, and the time to 25 minutes. Press Start/Stop to initiate preheating.

2. Line an 8-inch springform pan with baking paper and set aside.

3. In a medium bowl, whisk the butter, eggs, and vanilla extract. In another bowl, mix the cocoa powder, brown sugar, flour, and salt. Combine both mixtures until smooth. Fold in the pecans afterward and pour the mixture into the baking pan.

4. Once the Indoor Grill has preheated, open the lid and sit the baking pan on the base. Close the lid and bake for 20 to 25 minutes or until a toothpick inserted into the cake comes out clean.

5. When ready, transfer the cake to a wire rack to cool completely. Cut the cake into 2-inch squares and enjoy afterward.

Rating

Notes:

Bacon

Several recipes in this cookbook call for some bacon as an add-on. Since bacon can be eaten at all times of day in a full meal or as a snack we gave it its own special section.

101. Grilled Bacon

Level: Simple/Beginner | Function: Grill | Prep: 0 mins | Preheat: 8 mins | Cook: 9 to 11 mins | Makes: 2 – 4

INGREDIENTS:

5 bacon strips

DIRECTIONS:

1. Insert the grill grate into the Indoor Grill and close the lid. Select Grill, set the temperature to Low, and the time to 11 minutes. Press Start/Stop to begin preheating.

2. Once the Indoor Grill has preheated, open the lid and lay the bacon pieces on the grates. Close the lid and cook for 11 minutes without flipping.

3. When ready, transfer the bacon to a flat surface to cool and then chop or crumble afterwards.

Printed in Great Britain
by Amazon